Smart Food
for
Busy People

Stylish Food for New Zealanders

By Annabel Langbein

CULINARY INSTITUTE PRESS

CULINARY INSTITUTE
of NEW ZEALAND

**Culinary Institute Press is the imprint of
The Culinary Institute of New Zealand Ltd**

**Published by The Culinary Institute of
New Zealand Ltd
PO Box 99–068, Auckland, New Zealand
1993**

Production Team: Annabel Langbein
                      Sue Lyons
                      Chanda Cooper
                      Dawn Orr
Editor: Alison Mudford
Design and production: Moscow Design
Photography: Culinary Institute and
                      Cuisine Magazine
                      (see back page for
                      acknowledgments)
Illustrations and cover: Penny Kember

Typeset by Typocrafters Ltd, Auckland
Printed in Hong Kong

ISBN: 0-473-02228-1

Contents

The Storecupboard   6

Appetisers   10

Soup Glorious Soup   24

Salad Tactics   32

Pasta and Rice   42

Fast Fish   52

Poultry   74

Meat   88

Vegetarian   102

Desserts   114

Index   126

Introduction

We all like to eat well, but few of us welcome the idea of spending hours slaving over a hot stove. These days, thanks to a broad range of quality convenience foods and fresh ingredients, we can enjoy wonderfully memorable meals at home without having to spend much time in the kitchen.

Take a trip to the supermarket and browse along the shelves. I'm sure you will be surprised by the vast number of foodstuffs available — poppadoms and fresh curry spices from India; extra virgin olive oils, balsamic vinegars, Calamata olives and risotto rice from Italy; rice-paper wrappers and spicy chilli sauces from Thailand. These are just a few of the ethnic ingredients on offer. Consider, too, the growing number of wonderful New Zealand-made products — fabulous fresh stock from the Good Taste Company, fresh pasta and sauces such as pesto or tapenade, marvellous cheeses such as those produced by Kapiti Cheeses, gourmet meat bars with ready-to-cook stuffed roasts, marinated satays and clever little meat parcels. You don't need to be a gourmet or go to specialty food stores to find these foods because most large supermarkets now stock them.

New Zealand's fresh ingredients are unrivalled for flavour, freshness and quality. Increasingly, we are gaining international recognition for our ability to grow and manufacture premium-quality foodstuffs. Throughout the country, small concerns are flourishing, as demand grows for their "new" foods, such as fresh wasabi (Japanese horseradish), ewe's milk cheese, fresh truffles, Chinese vegetables, fresh herbs, cultured paua and olive oil. With such quality at our fingertips, we can create delicious effortless meals in next to no time.

This book celebrates the range and diversity of New Zealand food, with recipes and menus to suit every occasion — from busy midweek dinners to gala birthday celebrations. It is very much a book of food and meals that we eat at home every day, and it has evolved in response to the ingredients I find at my fingertips and the busy lifestyle that I'm sure many of us share in which we juggle children, partner, a busy career and friends. I have based my food around a formula that matches a well stocked pantry with fresh, good-quality produce. By following the guidelines in the chapter on "Stocking Up" you will find your cooking becomes even more streamlined and spontaneous. I have tried to include as many useful hints as possible too, to help you gain confidence in the kitchen.

The recipes are quick and easy to prepare and don't require a lot of skill or knowledge. However, they do require some care — and a basic respect for nature and the ingredient. The extra time you take to select top quality ingredients, and the care that you put into cooking, will make your food stand out. Its called "tasting the love". Take a little time, too, to set the stage for your meal. Simple table place-settings and glasses of delicious wine will provide a congenial atmosphere for great conversation.

This book would never have happened without the valuable assistance of a number of people. My grateful thanks to the team at the Culinary Institute — Sue, Chanda and Dawn who have worked tirelessly in the kitchen and in behind-the-scenes production to ensure the recipes are successful, that there are no mistakes and that we have achieved our goal. Thanks also to Julie Dalzell, whose magazine Cuisine has featured a number of the recipes and photographs in this book. Her, enthusiasm, support and great magazine have assisted me as a food writer and helped me develop my own food style over these last five years. Finally, thank you to my lovely husband Ted for his patience, support, good humour and friendship.

Annabel
September 1993

The Store Cupboard

A well-organised store cupboard is the key to success in dining well when time is at a premium. Stock your cupboard in three main ethnic styles — Mediterranean, Asian and Mexican and you will be able to create a tremendous variety of different tastes with little effort or forethought.

Taking a little time each week to prepare flavour bases such as crushed garlic, pestos, mayonnaise, vinaigrette dressing etc, further streamlines the cooking process and has a dramatic effect on the results — a quickly cooked piece of fish, for example, is elevated to restaurant status with a simple pesto garnish.

As long as you are well organised with the basics, you won't need to plan your menus day by day, rather you can take advantage of the freshest, best-quality produce as you find it.

Basic Pantry Supplies

Oils
- Pure olive — cooking and frying
- Virgin and extra virgin olive — salads and cold uses
- Corn or safflower — flavourless for Asian cooking and dressings
- Sesame — hot and cold uses

Vinegars
- Red and white wine — wine-based sauces and mustard dressings
- Balsamic — sweet aged vinegar, ideal for bitter greens, tomatoes or strawberries, and to finish casseroles and sautes
- Rice — mild, slightly sweet aromatic vinegar, ideal for cooking and cold uses
- Flavoured, eg tarragon, raspberry — use in sauces and dressings

Spices and Herbs
- Buy regularly and keep sealed for freshness
- Freeze soft herbs, eg basil, coriander, parsley, pureed with a little oil or made into pesto
- Freeze woody herbs, eg thyme, etc, on branch
- Purchase whole spices, eg cumin and coriander seeds, etc, toast and grind for more flavour
- Make up spice mixes eg fajita mix and curry mix, for easy, anytime use (see next page for recipes)

General

Asian
Soy sauce, hoisin sauce, black bean sauce, oyster sauce, fish sauce, chilli sauce (Thai brands), dried mushrooms, miso, wasabi, green curry paste, lemongrass, coconut milk, peanut butter, peanuts, cashews and sesame seeds, Japanese short grain rice, Thai long grain rice, eg basmati or jasmine, noodles, cornflour.

Canned Foods: Baby corn: for stir-fries, pies and frittatas
Straw and other canned mushrooms: for sauces, stir-fries, pasta sauces, soups
Water chestnuts: for stir-fries, salads and finger food

Key Herbs: coriander, mint, basil

Mediterranean
Honey, capers, olives, anchovies, tomato paste, pesto, tapenade, sundried tomatoes, prepared pasta sauce, tomatoes canned in juice, mustard, dried Italian pasta, semolina, polenta, risotto rice, parmesan cheese, mozzarella.

Canned Foods: Artichokes: for pasta sauces, casseroles, antipasto and salads
Beans and chickpeas: for soups, quick sautes, casseroles and salads
Bottled pasta sauce: all purpose
Canned tomatoes in juice: all purpose
Canned tuna: for pasta sauces, salads, frittatas, pies

Key herbs: basil, oregano, parsley, mint

Mexican
Taco sauce, Trappey's pepper sauce or tabasco, long grain rice, tortillas, tacos, fajita spice mix

Canned Foods: Chickpeas and beans: in fillings for tacos and tortillas.
Bottled Mexican taco sauce: spread onto fish or chicken and bake, mix with other flavourings for easy sautes and stir-fries

Key Herbs: coriander, oregano

Miscellaneous Storecupboard:
Stock — canned or packaged liquid stocks, root ginger, garlic, onions

Desserts
Meringues, brandy snaps, lady finger biscuits, biscotti, passionfruit pulp, apricot jam, pure vanilla, canned apple slices, canned lychees, canned mandarins, canned mangoes

On Hand in the Freezer

Bacon, chicken livers, fresh parmesan, frozen berries, frozen spinach, passionfruit pulp, pastry and filo pastry, smoked salmon, stocks

On Hand in the Fridge

Things to Make Regularly

Pureed Garlic: Peel, puree with olive oil and store in jar in fridge for up to 2 weeks. Keep a film of oil on top to stop mould from forming.

Roasted Garlic: Place whole heads of garlic in an oven dish, pour over about ½ cup olive oil and bake at 150°C for 35–45 minutes until tender. Allow to cool, then squeeze garlic puree out of husks. Mix with oil from cooking. Store in the fridge. This has a mild, sweet, nutty flavour that is a great addition to risottos, casseroles and spread onto crostini.

Prepared Ginger: Peel fresh root ginger and store in sherry, vinegar or white wine. Alternatively, store fresh whole piece of ginger in freezer.

Pesto: Make with seasonal soft herbs as available, pureed with olive oil, garlic and other flavourings as desired eg parmesan, nuts, sundried tomatoes etc. Over winter months try making pestos with parsley, coriander, rocket.

Basil Pesto: Into a food processor place about 2 packed cups basil leaves, 1 large clove garlic, peeled and sliced, ¾ cup good quality olive oil, ¼ cup parmesan cheese, salt and pepper to taste and optional ¼ cup toasted pinenuts or walnuts. Puree until they form a smooth paste. Store in the fridge or freeze in small containers.

Winter Parsley Pesto: Into a food processor place a large bunch of parsley without stalks, 2–3 cloves garlic, ¼ cup freshly grated parmesan cheese (store in freezer for anytime use), ¼ cup fresh shelled walnuts, ½ cup olive oil and a pinch each of salt and pepper. Puree until smooth, adjusting oil quantity until a smooth soft paste is achieved. Makes approximately 1 cup. Store in the fridge. Mix will keep for about 2 weeks. Spicy greens, such as rocket or watercress can be used in place of parsley.

Sundried Tomato Pesto: Into a food processor place ½ cup sundried tomatoes in oil, 2 cloves garlic, ¼ cup olive oil, handful of fresh parsley sprigs (optional) and a pinch each of salt and pepper. Puree until smooth. Nuts such as toasted almonds or walnuts, may be added as desired, thinning with more oil as needed. Makes ¾ cup. Store in the fridge. Without parsley, mix will keep indefinitely, with parsley it will last about 2 weeks.

Tapenade: Puree together 1 cup stoned Calamata olives, 1 tbsp crushed garlic, 4–6 anchovy fillets and 2 tbsp capers. Store in the fridge. Use in pastas, as a topping for steaks, mix into stuffings and fillings, use as a flavour boost for casseroles.

Roasted Peppers: This is an excellent method to preserve peppers when they are in peak supply. Wash red, yellow or green peppers and place in a 250°C oven for 15–20 minutes until they start to blister and brown. Remove and place in a covered container or plastic bag until cool enough to handle. Remove skin, seeds and pith from peppers under cold water. Slice peppers into strips and mix with a little olive oil. Refrigerate for 1 week or freeze.

Fajita Spice Mix: Into a jar place 5 tbsp paprika, 5 tbsp ground cumin, 3 tbsp garlic powder, 1½ tbsp each of chilli powder, brown sugar and salt and 2½ tsp chopped dry rosemary. Seal the jar and shake to combine. It makes enough for 2kg of meat or chicken. Allow 3 tablespoons per 500g meat. Store in a sealed jar.

Curry Spice: Mix 2 tbsp each of cumin seeds, coriander seeds and mustard seeds in a dry pan until they start to aroma. Grind and combine with 1 tbsp each of garlic powder, cayenne, turmeric, paprika and black pepper, and 2 tbsp each of ground cloves, cinnamon, fennel powder and cardomom powder.

Homemade Mayonnaise — see page 39

Aioli: Prepare homemade mayonnaise using olive oil, add 1 extra egg yolk and 1 tablespoon crushed garlic.

Quick Homemade Chicken Stock: Place 3–4 chicken carcasses or a couple of bags of chicken necks in a pot with 1 roughly chopped carrot, 1 unpeeled, halved onion, 3–4 peppercorns and enough water to cover by 4cm — no more. Bring to a boil and simmer for 45 minutes. Strain off scum. Strain stock, chill and remove fat. If desired, reduce stock and freeze in ice cubes.

Vinaigrette Dressing — see page 39

Croutons: Cut french bread diagonally and brush both sides with good olive oil or melted butter. Sprinkle with parmesan, herbs, garlic or garlic salt, etc, as desired. Bake in a single layer at 150°C for about 30 minutes until crisp. Store in an airtight container.

Suppliers

Most of the foodstuffs mentioned in this book can be obtained from supermarkets. Asian supplies can be located at any of the Asian Food Stores and supermarkets.

Other mail or direct order suppliers:

Fortex Meats — courier cuts service that includes meats, stock, sauces and spice mix Ph 0800 737 800

Kapiti Cheeses — mail order for Kapiti cheeses and other speciality cheeses Ph 0800 800 376.

The Culinary Institute — specialty imported foods such as risotto rice, Italian pasta, balsamic vinegar, virgin olive oils, venison stock, porcini mushrooms etc, available through mail order. Phone 09 307 3232.

Appetisers

Appetisers often take the place of a first course for a casual dinner or they can be a party in their own right. Either way we all want solutions that look impressive but don't take too much time to prepare. Finger food has a reputation for being fiddly because it's all in individual portions, but your efforts don't need to be complicated to ease everyone's hunger and make guests feel relaxed. A bowl of marinated olives and some garlic pita crisps make a great offering for pre-dinner drinks and provide a simple, delicious beginning to the evening's dining.

For parties allow about 5–6 different items and draw on ready-made supplies of flavour boosters such as pesto, tapenade, mayonnaise, vinaigrette etc for speedy preparations that provide lots of taste.

Vegetable Crudites with Basil Aioli Dip

Some Great Dunking

Most of us know how to whip together a tasty guacamole
(mix avocado flesh with lots of lemon juice, a dash of chilli and
salt and freshly ground black pepper to taste), but sometimes
you feel like something different — either for dipping into or dipping with!

Preparing Vegetable Crudites

Fresh vegetables make ideal dippers, they are light, nutritious and taste great with dipping sauces like sesame mayonnaise, basil aoili or any of the other dips featured here. A laden platter of assorted fresh vegetables and one or two delicious dips to dunk them into certainly stands in for a first course.

Baby potatoes, yams — scrub and simmer until just cooked then cool.
Snow peas, zucchini and asparagus — blanch for 30 seconds, then refresh in iced water.
Broccoli florets, cauliflower florets, green beans, broad beans — blanch for 1–2 minutes, then refresh in iced water.
Carrots, celery, peppers, green onions — place in iced water to crisp.
Mushrooms — marinate or serve raw.
Cherry tomatoes and cucumbers — serve raw.

Thai Shrimp Dip

Thai restaurants often serve this style of dip as an appetiser with prawn crackers.

Preparation Time: 5 minutes
Cooking Time: 5 minutes

250g shrimps
1 tsp crushed garlic
½ cup coconut cream
2 tbsp thickened cream or sour cream
½ tbsp hot chilli sauce
juice of ½ lemon
2 tbsp finely chopped fresh coriander, or basil or mint

Blend all the ingredients together to a semi-smooth puree. Serve with crackers, prawn crackers, poppadoms, garlic pita crisps or plain corn chips.

Cashew Nut Dipping Sauce

Preparation Time: 5 minutes

100g roasted salted cashew nuts
500g cream cheese
1 tbsp basil or other herb pesto
shake of black pepper
cream to thin

Blend all ingredients together. Thin to taste with cream. Makes about 2½ cups. Dip will store in the fridge for about 2 weeks.

Flavoured Mayonnaise
Use as a base the mayonnaise recipe on page 39

Sesame Mayonnaise
Mix together 1 cup mayonnaise, 1 tsp sesame oil, ¼ cup toasted sesame seeds, 1 tbsp sherry, 1 tbsp soy sauce.
  Makes about 1¼ cups. Dip will store in the fridge for about 1 week.

Basil Aoili Dip
Mix 1 cup mayonnaise with 1 egg yolk, 2–3 tbsp basil pesto and 1 tsp crushed garlic
  Makes about 1¼ cups. Dip will store in the fridge for about 1 week.

Tasty Dippers

Tortellini or ravioli
Buy ready-made ravioli or tortellini, cook and serve hot.

Poppadom Bites
Place a paper towel in microwave and lay 4–6 wedges of poppadom on it. Microwave for 1–2 minutes until poppadoms are bubbled and crisp. Repeat for the remaining poppadoms until all are cooked. Serve in a bowl with dip. Cooked poppadoms will keep crisp in a tightly sealed container for about 1 week. If they go limp they can be re-crisped in the microwave or in a 200°C oven.

Garlic Pita Crisps
Split large pita breads, cut into triangles and brush both sides of each piece liberally with garlic-flavoured oil (mix 2 tsp crushed garlic with ¾ cup olive oil). Place in a single layer on a baking tray and bake at 150°C for about 15 minutes until crisp.

Thai Chicken Skewers

Salmon Sates with Sesame Mayonnaise

Skewered foods are always popular and can be prepared with a wide variety of ingredients. To prevent charring soak wooden skewers for about 30 minutes prior to cooking. Any of these recipes can also be served as a first course or main if desired.

Salmon Sates with Sesame Mayonnaise

Preparation Time: 10 minutes
Cooking Time: 2 minutes

500g salmon, preferably in the piece
freshly ground black pepper
24 wooden sate sticks, soaked in water for 30
minutes

Remove bones and skin from the salmon and cut into strips 8cm long and about 1.5cm wide. Thread the salmon onto soaked sate sticks. Brush with melted butter and grind over black pepper. Place under a pre-heated grill (they don't need turning) for about 2 minutes. Serve hot, makes about 24. Accompany with sesame mayonnaise (see box for recipe).

Water Chestnut and Bacon Wraps

Preparation Time: 10 minutes
Cooking Time: 4–6 minutes

4–5 rashers rindless bacon
about ½ tsp garlic salt to sprinkle

230g tin water chestnuts, drained
24–26 toothpicks

Divide each rasher of bacon into 6×3cm strips. Sprinkle each piece of bacon lightly with garlic salt. Place a water chestnut in the centre of each piece of bacon and roll up to enclose. Secure with a toothpick. Grill for 2–3 minutes on each side or bake at 220°C for 5–6 minutes until golden. Makes about 24 wraps.

Thai Chicken Skewers

Preparation Time: 5 minutes
Cooking Time: 6 minutes

600g boneless, skinless chicken thighs, trimmed of
any fat and cut into 2cm pieces
1–2 tbsp green chilli paste or hot chilli sauce
1 tsp brown sugar
2 tbsp lemon or lime juice
wooden skewers, cut in half and soaked in cold
water for at least 1 hour

Combine the chicken with all other ingredients and leave to marinate in the fridge for at least 2 hours (or up to 6 hours). Thread onto skewers, allowing about 3 pieces per skewer. Place on a greased oven tray and press down gently with fingers to flatten chicken. Grill for 3 minutes each side until cooked through. Makes 40.

Serve with a peanut sauce made by heating peanut butter with crushed garlic, chilli sauce and enough water or coconut cream to form a thick cream consistency.

This recipe is good also as a chicken main course — serve about 6 pieces of chicken per skewer.

Crostini

Crostini, Italian for little crusts, originated in Italy as a clever way to use up stale bread. Traditionally these small toasts are grilled over an open fire, drizzled with olive oil, then topped with an array of mixtures that vary from something as simple as sliced tomato to more complex concoctions of mixed salads and meats.

Bruschetta, which is the traditional Italian workmans midday snack, applies the same principle but on a larger scale. A thick slab of country-style bread is grilled then rubbed with garlic, drizzled with good olive oil and sprinkled with sea salt. It can be eaten plain as such or embellished as desired like crostini. Serve crostini as appetisers and bruschetta for a casual impromptu lunch.

Menu

Friday Night Drinks After Work

Vegetable Crudite Basket with Basil Aoili and Sesame Mayonnaise

Crostini Platter

Whitebait Fritters or Herb and Feta Frittata

Fresh Fruit Platter

Preparation
1 Prepare basil aoili and sesame mayonnaise, prepare vegetables and refrigerate
2 Make crostini bases, prepare toppings
3 Assemble cheese and fruit platter
4 Assemble crostini
5 Assemble vegetable crudite basket
6 Prepare and cook whitebait fritters or frittata

Suggested Drinks
Champagne cocktails and Sauvignon Blanc

Chicken Liver Crostini

Chicken Liver Crostini

This hot crostini dish can be served as an appetiser or makes a delicious first course or light lunch.

Preparation Time: 10 minutes
Cooking Time: 5 minutes

250g chicken livers
1 tbsp flour
1 tbsp butter
1 ham steak, diced in 1cm cubes
¼ cup white wine or chicken stock
1 tsp lemon juice
salt and freshly ground black pepper

8 slices french bread
1 tbsp oil or butter to brown
squeeze of lemon juice

Trim any membranes from the chicken livers and cut in half. Dredge or dust them in flour, shaking off any excess. Heat the butter in a frypan, add the ham and brown quickly. Add the chicken livers. Cook for a minute over high heat to brown, then add the wine or stock, lemon juice and salt and pepper. Cover the pan and simmer for 5 minutes. Lightly brown the french bread slices on either side with a little oil in a frypan. Place on a serving dish and pour over the chicken liver mixture. Squeeze over a little extra lemon juice. Serve as an appetiser or with a green salad for lunch, supper or a light dinner. Serves 4.

Crostini and Bruschetta Topping Combinations

Crostini Bread Bases

Lightly toast small rounds (2–3cm thick) of french bread in a 180°C oven for about 20 minutes until crisp, then brush both sides liberally with olive oil. Alternatively, you can fry the bread rounds in a little olive oil until golden on each side. If not using immediately, store in an airtight tin and refresh in a warm oven.

Crostini and Bruschetta Topping Combinations
• Roasted pepper, roasted eggplant and anchovy
• Proscuitto, walnut pesto or cream cheese and olive paste
• Hummus, sundried tomato and pesto
• Smoked salmon, leeks, herbs and cream cheese
• Smoked salmon, tapenade, capers and red onion
• Spicy sausage, eggplant and pepper
• Roasted eggplant and pesto
• Sundried tomato pesto, marinated mozzarella and watercress
• Basil pesto and fresh mozzarella
• Basil pesto, sliced tomato and goat's cheese
• Tapenade, roasted pepper, mozzarella and cress
• Tapenade, hummus and roasted pepper strips
• Tapenade, smoked salmon and chives
• Tapenade, goats cheese and tomato
• Proscuitto, mozzarella and watercress
• Goat's cheese spread and watercress
• Smoked roe and dill
• Avocado mixed with shrimps and lemon juice

Herb and Feta Frittata

Frittatas are great food for portable occasions and parties, they can be prepared ahead of time and slice neatly. Frittatas can be prepared in a wide range of flavours, these two are amongst my favourites.

Preparation Time: 10 minutes
Cooking Time: 15 minutes

2 tbsp olive or cooking oil
2 potatoes, peeled and diced into 1cm chunks
1 tsp crushed garlic
3 tbsp chopped fresh herbs, eg thyme, oregano, parsley, chives, rosemary
100g crumbled feta cheese
6 eggs, lightly beaten
salt and freshly ground black pepper

Heat the oil in a frypan with a heat-proof handle. Add the potatoes and cook for 5–7 minutes or until the potatoes are just tender. Add the garlic and cook a further minute. Remove from the heat. Add the herbs and feta. Beat the eggs in a large bowl. Pour the potato mixture into the bowl, season and mix well to combined. Reheat the frypan. Pour the mixture into the pan and cook over low heat for 6–8 minutes. Place under a pre-heated grill and cook for 5 minutes or until golden brown and set. Leave in the pan until ready to serve. Turn out, cut into wedges and serve warm. Serves 4.

Smoked Salmon Frittata

Use 100g sliced smoked salmon or chopped smoked salmon pieces in place of feta and substitute fresh dill for other herbs.

Cheat's Mini Pizzas

Store-bought pizza bases make a great finger food — use biscuit cutters to cut bite-sized rounds before topping with your favourite pizza combination or either of these 3 delicious mixtures. Cut a 26cm prepared pizza base into small rounds of about 6cm diameter, cutting as closely as possible to each other to avoid waste. Place rounds on a lightly greased oven tray. Spread filling mixture over prepared bases. Bake at 220°C for 10–15 minutes or until pizza base is lightly golden brown.

Each of the following toppings will make enough for 1×26cm pizza base (about 13×6cm rounds)

Topping 1
Blend ½ cup cooked chopped spinach, squeezed dry, 80g blue cheese, crumbled and 2 tbsp sour cream.

Herb and Feta Frittata

Topping 2
Mix ⅔ cup prepared tomato pasta sauce, 100g chopped shrimps, ¾ cup grated mozzarella cheese, 1 tsp oregano.

Topping 3
Spread cooked pizza bases with sour cream, sliced smoked salmon and garnish with fresh dill.

Variation: serve filling in bread cases or vol au vent cases.

Herbed Black Olives

Preparation Time: 5 minutes

24 firm black olives
2 tbsp olive oil
2 tbsp mixed chopped fresh herbs, eg parsley, basil, thyme, oregano, rosemary
1 tsp crushed garlic
freshly ground black pepper

Lightly crush the olives with the flat edge of a knife. Combine with all other ingredients and serve in a bowl with toothpicks set on the side. Olives can be stored in this mixture in the fridge.

Optional Additions: Chillies, peppercorns, bayleaves

Fritters

Through the use of some eclectic flavourings fritters make great contemporary standby snack meals for impromptu guests. Rather than frying in butter or oil, use a heavy iron or non-stick pan and cook the fritters like pikelets — they taste better when cold and are much lighter on the palate.

Base Fritter Batter

Mix together until smooth ½ cup flour, ½ tsp baking soda, pinch salt and pepper, 1 egg and ¼ cup milk. With additions (see below) this mixture makes enough for about 16 mini fritters.

Cooking

Drop small spoonfuls of batter into a hot pan over medium heat to form small fritters. Brown on both sides. Serve hot or at room temperature.

Corn, Chilli and Coriander Fritters

Into prepared batter mix 2 cups corn kernels, ½ tsp chilli powder, ¼ cup chopped fresh coriander.

Smoked Fish Fritters

Into prepared batter mix 1 ½ cups flaked smoked fish, ¼ cup chopped fresh parsley or coriander and ½ tsp finely grated lemon rind.

Whitebait Fritters

Chinese whitebait has a lot less flavour than New Zealand whitebait. Add a little lemon juice if using it in these fritters.

Preparation Time: 5 minutes
Cooking Time: 4–5 minutes

400g whitebait, preferably New Zealand
1 egg
½ tsp finely grated lemon rind
1 tbsp flour
salt and freshly ground black pepper to season
butter for cooking

Combine the whitebait, egg, lemon rind, flour and salt and pepper. Melt a knob of butter evenly over the base of the pan. When the butter is sizzling, drop teaspoonfuls of the mixture into the pan. Cook for 1–2 minutes on each side or until golden brown. Makes 24 small fritters.

Cajun Pork Balls

Cajun Pork Balls

Meatballs cooked in the oven are less messy and less fatty. All meatballs cook really well this way.

Preparation Time: 20 minutes
Cooking Time: 15 minutes

800g leanish pork, diced
½ tsp garlic, crushed
2 tsp each of ground cumin and chilli powder
pinch of cayenne
2 tsp chopped fresh oreganum or 1 tsp dried
1 red pepper, finely diced
salt and pepper to taste

Place all ingredients in a blender and blend until the mixture is well combined and the pork is coarsely minced. Do not overprocess. Using wet hands, shape the mixture into balls the size of a large walnut. Place on a baking tray and bake at 200°C for 15 minutes until golden. Makes 45 small balls. Serve with guacamole or a spiked sour cream sauce made by mixing 250g sour cream, several shakes tabasco sauce, the juice of ½ lemon and ¼ cup finely chopped coriander.

Variation: Use chicken in placé of pork.

In The Raw

Sashimi, carpaccio, and tartare are all titles for seafood or meat that is served raw. The secret to success in serving raw proteins is in slicing or mincing the product extremely finely so that the taste is light and tender.

Venison Carpaccio

Preparation Time: 25 minutes plus 2–3 hrs freezing
Cooking Time: 3 minutes

400g venison hind leg fillet
1 tsp black peppercorns, crushed
¼ cup pistachio nuts, shelled and finely chopped
1 tbsp olive oil

Salad

about 40 assorted fresh lettuce leaves, eg red oak,
*   lambs lettuce, watercress, rocket*
1 red onion, very thinly sliced
3 oranges, peeled and segmented
1 avocado, cut in wedges

Dressing

¼ cup virgin olive oil
2–3 tbsp balsamic vinegar
1 tsp crushed garlic
pinch sugar

salt and pepper
garnish: sprigs of fresh herbs

Roll the meat in the crushed peppercorns and pistachio nuts. Heat the oil in a pan and quickly seal fillets on all sides. Wrap tightly in tinfoil and freeze for 2–3 hours until firm (or leave frozen until ready to use). Wash and dry all salad greens. Prepare the vegetables and fruit. Divide the salad greens and garnish between 6 plates. Slice the venison very thinly and arrange on plates. Spoon over dressing, garnish with a sprig of fresh herb and serve immediately. Serves 6.

Salmon Tartare

Chill fresh skinned, boneless salmon. Use a sharp heavy knife to mince finely. Don't let it become pasty. Mix through lots of lemon juice, some finely chopped capers, salt and pepper to taste and a light drizzle of olive oil. Serve with salad greens.

On The Half Shell

Shellfish on the half shell make a great freezer standby. Serve oysters raw with a tasty dressing or bake with a topping such as spinach and bacon. Mussels are delicious hot or at room temperature.

Mussels on the Half Shell with Pesto Vinaigrette

Preparation Time: 15 minutes
Cooking Time: 15 minutes

3 dozen fresh mussels, or cooked mussels on the half
*   shell*
2–3 tbsp pesto of your choice, eg basil or sundried
*   tomato pesto*
½ cup vinaigrette dressing
optional: ¼ cup chopped roasted red peppers

Steam the mussels open in ¼ cup water in a pot with a tight-fitting lid over high heat. Remove as they open. Take off the top shell. Mix together the pesto with the dressing, and freshly ground black pepper. Arrange the mussel shells on a plate and spoon over the pesto dressing. Garnish with optional peppers. Chill until ready to serve. Makes 36.

Chilled Oysters with Shinto Dressing

This light Asian styled dressing tastes beautiful with chilled, raw oysters. It will keep in the fridge for weeks.

Preparation Time: 5 minutes

2 dozen oysters on the half shell

Dressing

¼ cup rice wine vinegar
2 tbsp dry sherry

Chilled Oysters with Shinto Dressing; Mussels in the
Half Shell with Pesto Vinaigrette; Tuna Sashimi

½-1 tsp sugar
½ tsp fresh grated ginger or wasabi powder
½ tsp sesame oil

Garnish

Finely shredded blanched carrot and spring onion,
or blanched leek

Combine the sauce ingredients and chill. Just before
serving spoon a teaspoon of sauce over each oyster and
garnish with a little shredded vegetables. Makes 24.

Tuna Sashimi

For sashimi, choose fresh, quality fish, and slice very
thinly across the grain.

Preparation Time: 5 minutes plus 1 hour freezing

2 tbsp finely minced fresh root ginger blended to
    a paste with 3 tbsp oil
1 x 500g piece of fresh tuna (in one longish piece)
freshly ground black pepper

Dipping Sauce

¼ cup light soy sauce
2 tsp wasabi powder or paste

Spread the ginger paste all over the tuna, grind over
pepper and then wrap tightly in a piece of tinfoil. Freeze
until it is firm enough to slice easily. Slice very thinly
across the grain. Arrange slices in an overlapping
pattern onto a serving plate. Accompany with dipping
sauce, made by mixing together the soy sauce and
wasabi. Serves 6–8.

Variation: Prepare this dish using a fillet of beef or a
trimmed piece of venison denver leg.

Platters

The platter approach is a simple and stylish way to feed a large number of people at parties. Create platters of seafood, vegetables, meats and cheese or an antipasto mixture of different foods. Serve 5–7 different items on a large platter and accompany with dipping sauces.

Seafood Platter Ideas

Mussels on the Half Shell with Wine and Herbs

Scrub and remove beards from 2–3 dozen fresh mussels. Place in a large pot with ½ cup white wine, 2 tbsp finely chopped parsely and a little grated orange rind. Cover and steam, removing mussels as they open. Discard any that do not open. Remove the top shell of each mussel and spoon over the cooking juices. Chill until ready to serve. Mussels can be prepared up to 48 hours in advance — if more than 3–4 hours leave mussels in cooking liquid to prevent drying out.

Garlic and Lemon Squid

To be tender, squid either has to be cooked quickly or very slowly. Anything in between gives a very tough result.

Preparation time: 10 minutes
Cooking Time: 2 minutes

2–3 squid tubes
1 tsp crushed garlic
½ tsp finely grated lemon rind
2 tbsp olive oil
juice of 1 large lemon or lime
1 tbsp freshly chopped herbs, eg oregano, parsley, chervil
plenty of freshly ground black pepper

To prepare the squid, cut the tubes into thin rings, mix with garlic, lemon rind and olive oil. Leave to marinate for at least 15 minutes or up to 12 hours in the fridge. Heat a large heavy frypan or hot plate and quickly cook the squid over high heat for 1–2 minutes just until it whitens and is tender. Do not overcook. Mix through the lemon juice and chopped herbs and season to taste. Transfer to a container and refrigerate until ready to serve — squid can be cooked and chilled up to 48 hours before serving. Makes enough for 8–10 hors d'oeuvres or 4 first course plates.

Marinated Fish or Scallops

Preparation Time: 10 minutes plus 4 hours marinating

400g freshest fish fillets (scallops sliced in half or thirds)
¼ cup each of spiced vinegar and lemon juice
3 tbsp olive oil
¼ tsp tabasco sauce
optional: 12–15 fresh basil leaves, or coriander leaves finely chopped
salt and pepper to taste

Slice the fish into thin strips and place in a non-corrosive bowl or clean plastic bag with spiced vinegar and lemon juice. Leave to marinate in the fridge for at least 4 hours, stirring occasionally (up to 30 hours) or until fish has turned opaque. Mix through remaining ingredients, season to taste and serve. Makes enough for 8–10 hors d'oeuvres or 4 first course plates.

20

Seafood Platter

Sushi Rice Cakes

Preparation Time: 30 minutes plus 30 minutes soaking
Cooking Time: 10 minutes

1½ cups short grain rice
water to soak
6 tbsp rice vinegar or spiced vinegar
1 tbsp sugar
2 tsp salt
1 finely chopped spring onion
1 tsp finely grated orange or lemon rind
toasted black and white sesame seeds to roll

Wash the rice, then soak in cold water for 30 minutes. Drain off the soaking liquid and place the rice in a pot and cover to 1cm above its level with cold water. Bring to the boil rapidly, covered. Reduce heat to simmer for 10 minutes. In a separate pot or microwave bowl bring the vinegar, sugar and salt to the boil then remove from heat. Mix the seasoned vinegar through the rice with the spring onion and rind. Allow to cool. Use wet hands to shape handfuls of cooked seasoned rice into small cakes. Roll in toasted sesame seeds and arrange on a serving platter. Makes about 25 rice cakes. Rice cakes can be prepared up to 1 day in advance and stored in the fridge.

Smoked Salmon Rice Cakes

Mix 50g finely diced smoked salmon, 1 tbsp chopped fresh dill and ½ tsp finely grated lemon rind through the seasoned cooled rice and shape as above.

Chilli Smoked Mussel Rice Cakes

Mix 4 finely chopped smoked mussels and 1 tsp chilli sauce through the seasoned rice mixture.

Crispy Vegetable Rice Cakes

Add ¼ finely diced red pepper, ¼ cup finely diced cucumber and 2 tsp finely grated ginger to the seasoned rice mixture.

21

Antipasto Platters

Serve a selection of 4–7 items, to provide a variation of flavours, colours and textures.

Meats
Choose from thinly sliced smoked venison, thinly sliced smoked lamb, salamis and sausages, proscuitto folded into scrolls, thinly sliced smoked beef rolls, or a small bowl of pate.

Seafood
Choose from smoked mussels, mussels on the half shell, smoked mackerel, smoked salmon or a small bowl of smoked salmon or smoked fish pate.

Preserved Foods
Choose from pickled onions, gherkins, pickled peppers, pickled walnuts, olives and roasted red peppers.

Cheeses
Choose soft cheeses such as goats cheese, hipi iti, brie and fresh or marinated mozzarella.

Cheese and Fruit Platters

Serve 1–2 whole cheeses eg Kikorangi, a whole brie or hipi iti. Accompany with a variety of sliced fresh seasonal fruits and dried fruits to match, eg dried figs, apricots and pears and fresh berries, melon, kiwifruit, pineapple, stone fruit, pears, nashi and apples.

The Bar

The 70s and 80s were all about decadence and indulgence. We got so written off before dinner we hardly noticed what we ate. In the environmentally friendly, socially conscious 90s, we prefer to enjoy the company of our friends, good wine, good food and good conversation. The full bar, with its line up of Scotch, Gin, Brandy, Pernod, Dubonnet or whatever your fancy, and mixers to match, is less and less a feature of our lifestyles. These days we drink a lot more wine, and often, apart from water, wine is all you need to offer when friends come over for dinner. If you are in a party mood, a couple of fun cocktails will break the ice for the evening.

Kiwi Coladas

1 tub frozen kiwifruit juice, thawed or 500ml kiwifruit puree, chilled
½ can chilled coconut cream
200–250ml white rum
50ml cointreau
2 trays ice cubes

Blend all ingredients together. Makes 1.3 litres (enough for 5–6 cocktails).

60's Fruit Punch

1 litre cold tea, strained
2 litres orange and apple juice
1 litre grapefruit juice
1 litre ginger ale
1 litre lemonade
½ cup lime cordial
3 passionfruit (or 3 tablespoons pulp)
¼ cup chopped fresh mint
1 each orange, lemon and grapefruit
ice

Mix all together and decorate with sliced strawberries, oranges, lemon and mint leaves. Serves about 30.

Sludgy Margaritas
(by the blender full)

¾ cup fresh lime or lemon juice
¼ cup icing sugar
150ml tequila
50ml triple sec
3 trays ice cubes

Blend all ingredients together until they form a smooth puree. Serve immediately in a jug or pour into wide rimmed cocktail glasses that have had the rims dipped in lemon juice and then salt (optional). Makes 1 litre (enough for 4–5 cocktails.)

Trinidad Cooler

This light refreshing non-alcoholic drink makes great summer sipping.

generous splash of bitters
2 parts grenadine
1 part fresh lime juice
5 parts water
grate of fresh nutmeg

Combine all together and pour over crushed ice in a glass.

Champagne Cocktails

Champagne Cocktails

2 fresh peaches, stoned
½ cup peach schnapps or kirsch
2 cups ice
1 bottle sparkling wine

Blend peaches, schnapps and ice until smooth, then slowly add sparkling wine.

Variation: Omit peaches and ice and serve a nip of peach schnapps in the bottom of each glass of sparkling wine.

Variations on the Champagne Theme

Some of the less expensive methode champenoise wines are well suited to cocktails. Here are some great additions:
• dash of bitters, sugar lump and a strip of orange or lemon peel
• sugar lump, 2 dashes bitters, 1 tbsp Dubbonet, strip of lemon peel
• a little syrup from macerated tamarillos in sugar
• a tsp of cassis
• a little syrup made from cooked rhubarb and sugar
• a liqueur glass of brandy and a dash of curacao

Menu

An extravagant impromptu birthday party organised in the afternoon

Oysters on the Half Shell with Shinto Dressing

Mini Pizzas with Sour Cream and Smoked Salmon

Herbed Olives

Antipasto Platter

Whole Ham on the Bone with French Bread

Whole Brie with Fresh Fruits

Preparation
1 Prepare herbed olives
2 Prepare shinto dressing
3 Prepare mini pizza bases
4 Assemble antipasto platter
5 Arrange whole brie and fresh fruits
6 Slice french bread and place beside ham on the bone on a stand
7 Assemble and cook mini pizzas

Suggested drinks
Sludgy Margaritas, champagne, beer, lime and soda and fresh orange juice

Soup
Glorious Soup

There's nothing quite so heartwarming as a big bowl of soup, and after a long, hard day the 'bowl of soup and crusty bread' meal formula is hard to beat.

The creation of satisfying soups traditionally requires a lot of time, but thanks to ready-made stocks, pasta sauces, canned beans and chickpeas, and flavourings such as pesto, some delicious soups can be made very quickly.

Fridge leftovers — especially mashed potatoes, pumpkin or other root vegetables are very useful when it comes to soups. They are excellent thickeners, making white sauce unnecessary.

Spicy Sausage and Chick Pea Minestrone; Morrocan Pumpkin Soup; Smoked Ham Soup with White Beans and Mint

Moroccan Pumpkin Soup

When Joanne Weir came to teach at The Culinary Institute she made a slow-cooked version of this smooth and fragrantly spicy soup. I've adapted the recipe for busy cooks, with excellent results. This soup freezes well.

Preparation Time: 25 minutes
Cooking Time: 20–30 minutes

3 tbsp olive oil
1 large onion, chopped
¾ tsp each of paprika, turmeric and ground
*   coriander*
2 tsp ground cumin
800g to 1kg buttercup pumpkin or other nutty
*   pumpkin, peeled, seeded and cut into chunks*
4 carrots, peeled and coarsely chopped
6 cups chicken stock (or 2 cans chicken broth made
*   up to 6 cups with water)*
salt and freshly ground pepper to season
¼ cup fresh chopped coriander
Garnish: ½ cup creme fraiche

Heat the olive oil in a soup pot. Add the onion and spices and cook about 10 minutes until soft. Add the pumpkin and carrot and cook for 10 minutes. Add the chicken stock, salt and pepper. Bring to a boil, reduce heat and simmer uncovered for 20–25 minutes until carrots are soft. Add the fresh coriander and puree in batches in a blender until the soup is very smooth. If desired, the soup can be thinned with water or stock. Taste and season. Reheat, pour into bowls and garnish with creme fraiche. Serves 6.

Spicy Sausage and Chickpea Minestrone

This richly flavoured, chunky soup is a real cold beater.

Preparation Time: 10 minutes
Cooking Time: 12–15 minutes

2 tbsp oil
2 spicy sausages, diced eg Julia Colbasse
1 tsp crushed garlic
½ tsp chilli powder
500g jar tomato pasta sauce
3 cups chicken stock (or 1 can chicken broth made
*   up to 3 cups with water)*
2 cups water
2 cups chopped vegetables, eg pumpkin, leeks,
*   carrots, etc*
1 can chickpeas, drained and rinsed (or 1 ½ cups
*   cooked chickpeas)*
¼ cup herb pesto
2–3 tbsp grated parmesan cheese

In a soup pot heat the oil and cook the sausage, garlic and chilli for a few seconds. Add the tomato pasta sauce, chicken stock, water, vegetables and chickpeas. Bring to a simmer and cook for 12–15 minutes until the vegetables are tender. Just before serving mix in the pesto and parmesan and season to taste with salt and pepper. Serves 6.

Smoked Ham Soup with White Beans and Mint

You generally may think this type of soup takes hours to prepare but canned beans streamline the process without compromising the results. Follow it with a salad for a simple, elegant meal or special lunch.

Preparation Time: 20 minutes
Cooking Time: 20 minutes

1 tbsp olive oil
300g smoked ham, diced
1 medium onion, chopped
1 tbsp minced garlic
5 tomatoes, peeled, seeded, chopped (or 1 can
Italian plum tomatoes, chopped)
6 cups chicken stock (or 2 cans chicken broth made
*   up to 6 cups with water)*
2 cans white beans, drained and rinsed, eg soy beans
*   or lima beans*
6 parsley stems
6 mint stems, bruised
pinch dry thyme
2 bay leaves
salt and freshly ground pepper
6 tbsp fresh chopped mint

Menu
A Stylish Mid-Week Dinner

Moroccan Pumpkin Soup with Crusty Herb Bread
Fast-Baked Salmon with Pesto and Ribbon Zucchini

Tangelos in Caramel Syrup

Preparation
1 Make soup in advance and chill
2 Slice zucchini and blanch
3 Cut salmon into serving portions
4 Chill prepared dessert

To serve, roast salmon and heat zucchini with a little pesto.

Suggested Wine
A buttery oaked Chardonnay

Heat the oil in a soup pot and add the ham and onion. Cook about 8–10 minutes, until onion is soft. Add the garlic and continue to cook for 3 minutes until ham begins to turn golden. Add the tomatoes, chicken stock, beans and herbs. Simmer for 20 minutes. Lift out the parsley stems, mint stems and bayleaves. Season to taste and mix in the chopped mint. Serves 6.
N B: This soup reheats well.

Wild Mushroom Soup

This elegant soup gets a real boost of flavour from the addition of a handful of dried Chinese mushrooms. Dried mushrooms are readily available from Asian food stores and keep well in an airtight container.

Preparation Time: 40 minutes
(includes 30 minutes soaking time)
Cooking Time: 20 minutes

8 dried Chinese mushrooms
½ cup port
2 tbsp butter
1 tsp crushed garlic
300–400g field mushrooms, finely sliced
4 cups chicken stock (or 1 can chicken broth made
    up to 4 cups with water)
1 cup cream
black pepper and a pinch of nutmeg
¼ cup finely chopped parsley

Soak the Chinese mushrooms in port for at least 30 minutes, or until soft enough to slice finely. Lift out of the liquid, and slice, discarding stalks. Return to the liquid and reserve. Heat the butter and cook the garlic for a few seconds. Add the field mushrooms and cook until dry and just starting to brown. Add the soaked mushrooms and their liquid and cook until dry. Add the chicken stock and simmer for 15 minutes over a low heat. Mix in the cream (or leave clear and thicken with 2 tsp arrowroot in a paste with a little water) and bring to a simmer. Season well with black pepper, nutmeg and mix in the chopped parsley. Serves 4.

Variation: for a special occasion use an equal quantity of dried ceps or 2–3 dried morels in place of dried Chinese mushrooms.

Dried Mushrooms

Dried mushrooms have an intense flavour unmatched by fresh. Chinese dried mushrooms are much cheaper than European ceps and morels and, although their flavour is different, can be substituted wherever dried mushrooms are used. Store dried mushrooms in a sealed container. To use, soak in wine, port or water until pliable. Remove and discard the stems of Chinese mushrooms, slice and add with the soaking liquid.

Mad On Mussels

Apart from their wonderful taste and speed of cooking, mussels are also a good source of calcium and protein. To check for freshness either tap lightly or run under cold water. Mussels that do not close should be discarded. Conversely, when cooking discard any that do not open.

Thai Mussels with Chilli and Coriander

This substantial spicy brew falls into the category of a soup dinner that only requires some type of bread accompaniment and, if desired, a salad or dessert to follow. The recipe doubles easily.

Preparation Time: 10 minutes
Cooking Time: 15 minutes

16–20 fresh mussels
1 large onion, finely diced
1 tbsp oil
1 tsp crushed garlic
2 tbsp hot chilli sauce (Thai brand)
1 tin coconut cream
2 cups water
2 tbsp fresh chopped coriander

Scrub the mussels under running water, discarding the beards. Reserve. Cook the onion in oil in a soup pot over low heat until soft. Add the garlic and chilli sauce and stir over heat for a minute. Add the coconut cream, water and cleaned mussels, cover tightly and boil until the mussels start to open, removing them as they do. Mix in the coriander just before serving. Serve 4–5 mussels per person in a deep bowl and spoon over the broth. Garnish with extra fresh coriander. Serves 4 as a soup and 2–3 as a main course.

Mexican Mussel Soup

Mexican Mussel Soup

Preparation Time: 5 minutes
Cooking Time: 20 minutes

1kg fresh mussels
½ cup water
1 tbsp oil
2 medium onions, finely chopped
2 tsp ground cumin
1 tsp garlic
½ tsp–1 tsp chilli powder (to taste)
2 tbsp tomato paste
400g tin tomatoes in juice
3 cups chicken stock (or 1 can chicken broth made
  up to 3 cups with water)
200g mixed green vegetables, eg broccoli, beans,
  cauliflower, chopped into bite-sized pieces
1 cup grated cheese
salt and freshly ground black pepper
pinch cayenne
garnish: corn chips

Scrub the mussels and steam in a large saucepan with
the water until they open. Remove from the shells and
cut up the flesh, saving all the cooking juices. Reserve.
Heat the oil in a large saucepan, add the onion, cumin,
garlic, chilli powder and tomato paste. Cook for 5
minutes until the onion starts to soften. Add the
tomatoes, stock, juice from the mussels and vegetables.
Cover and simmer for 10–15 minutes until the vegetables are tender. Mix in the cheese and cooked
mussels. Season to taste with salt, pepper and a pinch
of cayenne. Garnish with corn chips. Serves 4.

Amercian Mussel and Corn Chowder

This chunky, substantial chowder makes a great winter
meal. Use chilli or garlic flavoured mussels as a
variation.

Preparation Time: 10 minutes
Cooking Time: 20 minutes

1 tbsp butter
1 large onion, diced
2 stalks celery, finely diced
2 medium potatoes, diced in 1cm cubes
3 cups chicken stock or 1 can chicken broth made up
  to 3 cups with water
1 tsp dried thyme
2 bayleaves
1 cup whole kernel corn, drained
200g mussels smoked, finely chopped
1 tbsp cornflour mixed with 2 tbsp sherry or water
2 cups hot milk
¼ cup chopped parsley
salt and black pepper to taste

In a large saucepan heat the butter and cook the onion
and celery over a low heat the until onion is soft. Add
the potato, stock, thyme, bayleaves, corn and smoked
mussels and simmer over low heat until the potato is
cooked (about 10 minutes). Mix in the cornflour paste
until it thickens, then add the hot milk and parsley.
Allow to simmer for 3–4 minutes. Season to taste with
salt and pepper.
Serve with hot, crisp bread. Serves 6.

West Coast Mussel Soup

Robin Morrison was famous not only for his marvellous
photography but also for his cooking, including this
simple yet excellent mussel soup.

Preparation Time: 5 minutes
Cooking Time: 10 minutes

2kg mussels in shell
2 cups water
2 tsp crushed garlic
1 cup white wine
1 cup cream
freshly ground black pepper to taste
¼ cup finely chopped parsley

Scrub the mussels and steam in a large lidded pot with
the water, removing as they open. Remove from shells,
saving all the cooking juice. Puree the mussels and
garlic in batches. Place the puree in a pot with reserved
cooking juices, wine and cream and bring to a simmer.
Season to taste with lots of pepper. Stir through the
parsley. Serves 6.

Miso Soup; Tom Yum Soup

In The Can

10 Minute Soups using Canned Stocks

Short order soups require decent stocks and flavourings — stock
powder mixed with water simply won't deliver the same results.

Tom Yum Soup

This Thai favourite makes a quick, light first course.

Heat 1 can chicken broth made up to 3 cups with water
(or 3 cups homemade chicken stock). Add 2 tbsp lemon
juice, ½–1 tsp dried chilli flakes (or finely chopped dried
chilli to taste), 1 tbsp minced lemon grass (or 1 tsp finely
grated lemon rind), 2 tbsp fish sauce and 2 bay leaves.
Simmer for 5 minutes. Add 150g of either shrimps,
thinly sliced chicken or thinly sliced beef and simmer
1 minute more. Mix in 2 tbsp chopped fresh coriander.
Stand for a minute before serving. Makes 2 servings.
Recipe doubles easily.

Canned beef or chicken consomme make a good
stock substitute. Other good flavour boosters to
keep on hand for quick, tasty soups include:

- Venison Glace (concentrated venison stock)
  made by the Good Taste Company is a great beef
  stock substitute (see page 9 for stockists)
- Canned tomatoes and pasta sauce
- Miso
- Packaged soup bases, eg tom yum
- Canned beans and chickpeas
- Bacon, spicy sausages and salami

Straciatella Soup

This Italian soup is a surprising contrast of yellow and
bright green. Frozen spinach can be used if desired
— thaw and squeeze out excess moisture.

Heat 1 can chicken broth made up to 3 cups with water
(or 3 cups homemade chicken stock). Mix in 1 cup
cooked chopped spinach, and while soup is boiling
whisk in 2 lightly beaten eggs with a fork, breaking eggs
into thin threads. Season with ¼ cup grated parmesan
cheese and salt and pepper to taste. Season well. Makes
2 servings. Recipe doubles easily.

Miso Soup

This light, head clearing broth is very nutritious. Add
vegetables, instant noodles and a protein of your choice
to turn it into a speedy meal.

Heat 1 can chicken broth made up to 3 cups with water
(or 3 cups homemade chicken stock). Add 1 tsp dry
sherry, a small handful of dried seaweed and 1 tbsp
soy sauce. Simmer for 5 minutes. Mix in 1 tbsp miso
paste and 2 sliced spring onions and heat without boiling
until the miso has dissolved. Makes 2 servings. Recipe
doubles easily.

Bread Complements

Everyone loves homemade bread but often it's overly time consuming to prepare. For those who have the time I've included a lovely recipe for foccacia bread, which freezes well. Quickbreads, like cornbread don't require rising or kneading but need to be eaten fresh. Croutons on the other hand take no time to prepare and keep well.

Texan Corn Bread

Preparation Time: 15 minutes
Cooking Time: 60–65 minutes

2 large eggs
1¾ cups milk
¼ cup oil
1 tsp chilli paste
310g tin whole kernel corn, drained (or 1½ cups corn)
  kernels)
optional: ½ red pepper, diced
2 cups each of coarse cornmeal and flour
3 cups grated tasty cheese
2 tsp baking powder
½ tsp baking soda
1–1½ tsp salt

Combine the eggs, milk, oil, chilli, corn and optional pepper. In a separate bowl combine the dry ingredients and cheese. Mix in the liquid ingredients until just moistened — do not overmix. Turn into a large greased and lined loaf pan. Bake at 180°C for 60–65 minutes, or until a skewer comes out clean. Serve the same day or freeze.

Croutons

Cut french bread into diagonal slices approximately 1cm thick. Spread with any of the following toppings. Place on a baking tray and bake at 190°C for 12–15 minutes, until light golden brown. The croutons should be lightly crisp, without disintegrating when eaten.

Tapenade Croutons
Spread one side of the bread slices with tapenade (see page 9 for recipe).

Pesto Croutons
Spread one side of the bread slices with pesto. (see page 9 for recipe).

Garlic Oil Croutons
Combine crushed garlic with olive oil. Brush both sides of the bread slices.

Fried Croutons
Cut 1.5cm-thick slices from a whole loaf of bread. Remove crusts and cut into 1.5cm squares. Heat 2cm of olive oil in a heavy-based pan. Cook the croutons for 2–3 minutes, tossing in the oil until light golden brown. Drain on paper towels.

Focaccia Bread

Preparation Time: 10 minutes + 1½ hours rising
Cooking Time: 35–45 minutes

1½ tsp salt
625g high grade flour (4½ cups)
1 tbsp dry yeast
1½ cups lukewarm water
1 tsp sugar
½ cup olive oil
¼ cup pitted black olives, chopped
extra flour for kneading as required
2 tsp sea salt
water to brush the top

Combine the salt and flour in a bowl. Dissolve the yeast with the sugar in ½ cup of the lukewarm water, then mix in the rest of the water. Whisk in about 1½ cups of the flour, ½ cup at a time then mix in the oil and the olives.

Leave to rise until doubled in bulk (about ¾ of an hour).

Turn onto a floured bench and knead in the extra flour, kneading until the mixture is smooth, very elastic, and free from air. Flatten into a roasting dish approximately 22×30cm, so that dough is 2cm thick. Slash or mark as desired, cover with a just-damp clean cloth and leave to rise in a warm place until doubled in bulk (about ¾ hour). Brush lightly with a little olive oil and sprinkle with sea salt. Bake in a preheated 220°C oven for 15 minutes, then reduce heat to 200°C and cook a further 20–25 minutes until loaf sounds hollow when tapped. After 15 minutes cooking, brush loaf with water, and repeat this twice to give it a thick crisp crust. This bread freezes well and once thawed can be reheated successfully with great success. Makes 1 large loaf.

Note: The dough can be made in a blender. Knead in the olives by hand so they remain whole.

Pizza with Rocket, Peppers, Olives, Sundried Tomatoes and Mozarella. Right: Smoked Salmon, Sour Cream and Watercress

Pizza Pizza

Pizza has come a long way since the ham and pineapple offerings of my youth. Good pizza has a crisp crust, not too much topping and it is very moreish.

Pizza Base

2 tsp sugar
1⅓ cups warm water
2 tbsp dry yeast
4 cups high grade flour
2 tsp salt
2 tbsp olive oil

To prepare the base, dissolve the sugar in the warm water. Sprinkle the yeast over the water and stand in a warm place for 10 minutes. Combine the flour and salt in a mixing bowl. Stir in the yeast mixture and oil until well combined. Knead on a lightly floured surface for 10 minutes until smooth. Place the dough in a lightly oiled bowl. Cover and stand in a warm place for 30 minutes or until the dough has doubled in size (or microwave the dough at the lowest power setting for 5 minutes, then stand for 10–15 minutes). Push a clenched fist into the middle of the dough to deflate and turn onto a lightly floured surface. Roll out to 2×28cm rounds. Sprinkle with toppings as desired. Bake at 200°C for 25–30 minutes. Makes 2×28cm pizza bases.

Topping Ideas

- crumbled spicy sausage, mozzarella and coloured peppers
- sundried tomato pesto, coloured peppers, cherry tomatoes, basil and garlic oil
- coloured peppers, blue cheese, salami and cherry tomatoes
- peppers, capers, olives and mozzarella
- roasted onions, kikorangi, sage and mozzarella
- roasted onions, feta cheese, herbs and mozzarella
- tapenade, wilted greens (spinach, watercress or rocket), red peppers, olives and mozzarella (pictured)
- basil pesto, roasted eggplant, tomatoes and mozzarella
- leeks, goat cheese and toasted pine nuts
- fresh mozzarella, herbs and extra virgin olive oil
- creme fraiche, mozzarella, smoked salmon and watercress
- sundried tomato pesto, roasted eggplant slices and grated parmesan cheese
- sundried tomato pesto, salami, olives and feta
- garlic oil, tomato sauce, roasted eggplant slices and mozzarella
- harvati cheese, stewed artichoke hearts, cooked garlic and ham

Salad Tactics

Remember when a salad consisted of a few limp lettuce leaves or some shredded cabbage, slatherings of store-bought salad dressing and the token slice of tomato or cucumber as garnish? Today's salads aren't just interesting to eat and beautiful to look at, they often make a wonderful meal in themselves that's packed with great tastes and good nutrition.

Paw Paw, Avocado, Pepper and Prawn Salad; Salad of Roasted Fresh Walnuts and Grilled Hipi iti; Thai Smoked Chicken Salad

The Salad as a Meal

For success with salads as stand-alone meals or first courses include ingredients that produce a variety of fresh colours, textures and flavours. Ensure the greens are dressed before the 'garnishes' are added.

Salad of Roasted Fresh Walnuts and Grilled Hipi iti

New Zealand's first ewe's milk cheese, Hipi iti has a wonderful flavour and smooth firm texture which grills well.

Preparation Time: 10 minutes
Cooking Time: 6 minutes

1 cup fresh shelled walnuts
¼ cup virgin olive oil
2 cloves garlic, crushed
2 large bunches freshest watercress, washed and stems removed (or 2 gourmet lettuces)
8–10 baby yellow or red tomatoes, halved
2 tsp balsamic vinegar or lemon juice
3 rounds of Hipi iti cheese, cut in half through the middle
black pepper
garnish: julienne of spring onion tops

Cook the walnuts in olive oil over gentle heat until just golden, taking care not to burn. Add the garlic and cook for a few seconds. Allow to cool. Wash and dry salad greens and tomatoes and toss through with olive oil and walnut mixture. Mix in balsamic vinegar or lemon juice. Place the cheese slices on baking tray and grill under high heat for 2–3 minutes until cheese is just starting to melt and browns. They will look like poached eggs. Divide salad greens, walnuts and tomatoes among 6 plates and top each with a round of hot cheese.
Serves 6 as a first course.

Caesar Salad

This classic salad has won new-found fame throughout most bistros and grills in the Western world. It's probably the most moreish green salad you'll ever come across. If you want more of a meal, top with a lightly poached egg.

Preparation Time: 10 minutes
Cooking Time: 30 seconds

20–25 leaves romaine, Cos or other crisp lettuce

6 anchovies
½ tsp crushed garlic
½ cup olive oil
2 tbsp lemon juice
optional: 2 tbsp cream
2 eggs, coddled (30 seconds in boiling water)
1½ cups crisp garlic or tapenade croutons or 12 french bread croutons (see page 39)
¼ cup grated parmesan cheese
10 grinds black pepper

Wash and carefully dry the lettuce then tear into bite-sized pieces, discarding the base stems. Place in a salad bowl. Mince the anchovies with the garlic and mix in the oil, lemon juice and lightly coddled eggs to form a dressing — this can be done in a jar or blender. Toss the dressing through the greens just before serving, then top with the croutons and cheese. Serve immediately. Serves 4–6.

Thai Smoked Chicken Salad

Cooked chicken of any kind can be used in this excellent layered salad. Add extra salad ingredients as available.

Preparation Time: 25 minutes
(includes 20 minutes soaking)

(¼ packet) 50g vermicelli rice noodles, soaked in warm water for about 10 minutes until pliable
1 large crisp lettuce or a mixture of lettuce and spinach, finely shredded
2 carrots, shredded and mixed with 1 tsp sugar
½ red onion or 2 spring onions, thinly sliced
½ cup toasted peanuts, chopped
¼ cup finely chopped fresh coriander or mint (or a mixture of both)
flesh of 2 smoked chicken breasts (shredded into bite-sized pieces, or 1 whole roasted chicken)

Dressing
¼ cup Vietnamese sauce
1 tsp sugar
juice of 1 lemon
1 tsp hot chilli sauce

Layer all the salad ingredients onto a large salad platter. Combine dressing ingredients and pour over. Serves 6.

When Mayonnaise or Guacamole Curdles

Simply blend in a little hot water until the mixture comes together again. An emulsion is formed by oil and water and if there is not sufficient water it will separate.

Avocado, Bacon and Banana Salad
Caesar Salad

Avocado, Bacon and Banana Salad

This combination of bacon, avocado, banana and spinach is easy to construct and tastes a million dollars.

Preparation Time: 10 minutes
Cooking Time: 5 minutes

1 large bunch spinach leaves or other greens, washed
3 rashers bacon, diced and cooked until crisp
2 firm bananas, sliced thinly on the diagonal
1 large firm but ripe avocado, cut into wedges

Dressing

¼ cup olive oil
2 tbsp lemon juice
½ tsp crushed garlic
½ tsp sugar
salt and freshly ground black pepper

Strip spinach leaves from their stems and break into bite-sized pieces. Shake the dressing ingredients together in a jar. To assemble the salad, toss the spinach leaves in three quarters of the dressing and lightly mix through about half of the bacon, banana, and avocados. Arrange on a salad platter, garnish with the remaining ingredients and spoon over the rest of the dressing. Serves 4.

Paw Paw, Avocado, Pepper and Prawn Salad

The addition of prawns into this delicious recipe transforms it from a side-salad into a meal. You could also use grilled chicken. Omit the protein when serving this salad with main-course grills and meats.

Preparation Time: 10 minutes

½ large firm but ripe pawpaw, peeled, seeded and
* sliced*
1 avocado, cut into chunks
1 large red pepper, sliced in thin strips
¼ cup lime juice
2 tbsp fresh root ginger, cut into fine strips
1 bunch chives cut in 2cm lengths
1 bunch spinach, washed, dried and stems removed
2 tbsp oil
1 tbsp lemon juice
optional: 400–500g cooked prawns

Toss the paw paw, avocado and pepper with the lime juice, ginger and chives. Dress the spinach with a little oil and some of the lime juice from the paw paw. Arrange on a platter, pile the pawpaw and avocado mixture on top. Garnish with the optional prawns. Serves 8–10 as a side-salad or 4 as a first course.

Oriental Pork Salad

Oriental Pork Salad

This fresh light salad can also be made with leftover cold roast pork, in which case the marinating procedure is omitted. Pork benefits from being placed in a marinade for several hours before cooking to soften and moisten it. The salad may be dressed with a simple french dressing or this nutty vinaigrette.

Preparation Time: 15 minutes plus marinating
Cooking time: 20 minutes

500–600g pork fillet (trimmed) or 500–600g thinly sliced cold roasted pork
Marinade
1 tbsp honey
1 tbsp fresh finely chopped ginger
2 tbsp sherry or port
Salad
½ telegraph cucumber, peeled and sliced into long thin strips
⅔ cup cape gooseberries
3 spring onions, sliced diagonally
handful of chives
½ cup walnut halves
Dressing
¼ cup walnut halves
1 tbsp honey

1 tsp finely chopped ginger
⅓ cup oil
⅓ cup orange juice
1 tbsp lemon juice

Combine the marinade ingredients and spread over the raw pork fillets. Leave to marinate for at least 4 hours at room temperature or overnight in the fridge. Dry the pork with paper towels, brown quickly in a buttered frying pan and then roast at 220°C for 15–20 minutes until the pork is cooked to medium doneness (70°C internal temperature). Remove from the oven and allow to cool. When cool, refrigerate until firm enough to slice very thinly. Slice the meat into paper thin shreds, combine in a salad bowl with the sliced cucumber, cape gooseberries, spring onion slivers and walnut halves. Blend the dressing ingredients together until well incorporated and toss through salad. Serve immediately. Serves 4–5.

Raw Energy Salad

This salad makes a great lunch or summer meal. If you feel like adding some more substance, try cooked chicken or tuna.

Preparation Time: 10 minutes

1 bunch fresh spinach, leaves washed and stems removed
¼ cup vinaigrette dressing (or a little oil and lemon juice)
2 tbsp chopped fresh herbs
1 large red pepper, cut into thin strips
1 crisp carrot, peeled and shredded
1 pkt snow pea shoots
1 small red onion, thinly sliced
¼ pawpaw or rock melon peeled, seeded and cut into segments
1 bunch radishes, quartered, sliced thinly
optional ½ cup raw almonds
juice of ½ lemon
½ tsp sugar
freshly ground black pepper to taste
Avocado Dressing

Combine in a blender the following: flesh of 1 avocado, the leaves from a large sprig of mint, ¼ cup water, the juice of ½ lemon, dash of tabasco, salt and pepper to taste.

Toss the spinach leaves with the vinaigrette dressing. Arrange on a big platter and sprinkle over the chopped herbs. Toss the other vegetables with lemon juice, sugar and pepper and pile on top. Serve each salad with a scoop of avocado dressing on top. Serves 2 as a meal or 4 as a starter.

Alternatively use Goddess Dressing on page 108.

Thai Beef Salad

Preparation Time: 10 minutes plus cooling
Cooking Time: 5–6 minutes

400g good quality beef steaks, cut about 2cm thick,
* fat removed*
salt and pepper
2 tsp sesame oil
2 tbsp soy sauce
juice of ½ lemon
1 tbsp fish sauce
1 cup bean sprouts

300g fresh spinach, washed, stalks removed and
* shredded finely*
2 tbsp toasted sesame seeds
garnish: fresh coriander

Season the steaks with salt and pepper. Pan fry the steaks over a high heat in sesame oil until medium-rare. Remove from heat and allow to cool in the pan. When cool, slice thinly across the grain into matchsticks and mix with all other ingredients, except the beansprouts, spinach, sesame seeds and coriander. Arrange a pile of spinach and beansprouts on top of each serving plate and pile the meat on top. Sprinkle with sesame seeds and coriander. Serves 4.

Salad Partners

The following salad recipes make great partners to grilled meats, curries, oven bakes and pasta dishes. Vary according to your own taste preferences and seasonal availabilities.

Spinach and Feta Salad with Olives and Croutons

Preparation Time: 10 minutes
Cooking Time: 10–12 minutes

2 tbsp lemon juice
¼ cup olive oil
salt and plenty of freshly ground black pepper
1 large bunch spinach, leaves washed and dried,
* stems removed*
150g feta cheese, crumbled
½ cup black olives
2 spring onions, sliced
2–3 tomatoes, cut into quarters
12–15 croutons (see page 00), or half a packet of
* garlic bagel chips*

Mix the lemon juice and olive oil, season with salt and pepper and toss through the spinach leaves. Divide the spinach among 4–6 salad plates. Top with feta, olives, spring onions, tomatoes and croutons. Serve immediately. Serves 4–6.

Brie, Bacon and Avocado Salad

Preparation Time: 10 minutes
Cooking Time: 4 minutes

Brie, Bacon and Avocado Salad

3 rashers bacon, diced
20–30 assorted lettuce leaves (or spinach), washed
* and dried*
125g brie, sliced into thin wedges
1 just ripe avocado, diced
12–18 croutons
optional: 4 boiled quails eggs or poached eggs

Dressing

½ cup vinaigrette dressing
½ tsp crushed garlic
1 tsp dry mustard
1 egg yolk
optional: 2 tsp balsamic vinegar
salt, black pepper and a pinch of sugar

Cook the bacon until crispy (use some of the oil for dressing if bacon is very lean). Combine the dressing ingredients in a jar. Mix the dressing through the salad greens and divide among 6 plates. Top with the bacon, brie, avocado, croutons and optional halved quail eggs. Serve immediately. Serves 6.

Variation: Add strawberries and blanched green beans

Marinated Mozzarella with Baby Tomatoes and Pickled Walnuts

Marinated mozzarella is a wonderful addition to salads and pasta dishes. This pretty fresh salad makes an ideal first course or accompaniment for grilled or barbecued meats.

Preparation Time: 10 minutes plus marinating

4 fresh bocconcini or 200g ball of fresh mozzarella
about 1 cup extra virgin olive oil
2 tsp garlic, roughly crushed
2 sprigs rosemary, about 5cm each
2 bay leaves
1 punnet baby tomatoes, halved
4 pickled walnuts, cut finely
1 bunch of rocket or watercress

Slice the mozzarella thinly and mix with the oil, garlic, rosemary and bay leaves, topping up with more oil if necessary to make sure cheese is fully covered. Leave to marinate for at least 8 hours or for up to a week in the fridge, turning occasionally. To assemble salad, lift cheese from oil, and mix with tomatoes. Arrange slices of cheese and tomatoes in an overlapping pattern onto 4 small plates. Drizzle over a little of the oil and sprinkle with pickled walnuts. Garnish at the side with rocket leaves, watercress or sprigs of fresh soft herbs. Serves 4.
N B: The leftover oil is delicious in salads and sauces

Asparagus Salad with Cashews, Bacon and Oranges

Preparation Time: 15 minutes
Cooking Time: 5 minutes

about 16–20 assorted lettuce leaves, eg red endive, etc
20–24 asparagus spears
4 oranges
¾ cup toasted cashew nuts
optional: 1 avocado, sliced
2 rashers bacon, finely diced and cooked until crisp

Dressing

½ cup fresh orange juice
2 tbsp olive oil
salt, pepper and a pinch of sugar

Wash and dry the salad greens. Snap ends from the asparagus and cook in boiling water for 2 minutes. Drain and cool in cold water. Peel and segment the oranges. To assemble salad, combine the dressing

ingredients and toss half through the spinach. Arrange salad greens on a large salad platter, top with asparagus, orange segments, optional avocado and cashews. Sprinkle over hot bacon. Spoon the rest of the dressing over the top. Serves 4.

Mixed Green Salad with Roasted Walnuts

Preparation Time: 10 minutes

6 large handfuls salad greens, including rocket and/or cress
⅓ cup virgin olive oil
1 cup fresh walnut pieces
2 tbsp red wine vinegar
pinch each mustard powder and sugar
salt and freshly ground black pepper

Wash and dry the salad greens. Heat the oil in a heavy pan or pot and gently fry the walnut pieces until they start to turn golden. Cool, then mix in the red wine vinegar, mustard powder, sugar and salt and pepper. Mix through the walnuts to combine, then toss through the salad greens. Serves 6.

Salad dressing fixings

The Art of Making a Good Salad

1 Select the freshest salad greens (preferably an assortment)
2 Add interest with ingredients that provide contrasts of texture, flavour and colour.

3 Wash and dry salad greens. Store in a bag in the fridge if not using immediately).
4 Dress greens in a large bowl and transfer to a serving bowl to serve at once.

Basic Vinaigrette Dressing

3 tbsp spiced vinegar or lemon juice
½ cup extra virgin olive oil
½ tsp each mustard and sugar
salt and pepper

Combine all ingredients in a jar. Store in the fridge.

Variations
Garlic Dressing: add 1–2 tsp crushed garlic
Italian Dressing: add 2 tbsp dry vermouth and 2 tbsp fresh chopped herbs
Walnut Dressing: blend in ½ cup fresh walnuts

On the Spot Dressing for Greens:

Drizzle a little olive oil over washed and dried salad greens. Squeeze over the juice of a lemon, add a pinch of salt, sugar and black pepper and toss all together.

The Best Mayonnaise

Creamy, rich and lemony, this versatile mayonnaise is an all-time favourite.

Preparation Time: 15 minutes

2 tsp dry mustard
1 tsp salt
½ tsp white pepper
1 tsp sugar
¼ cup lemon juice
½ tsp finely grated lemon rind — no white pith
3–4 egg yolks
about 2½ cups salad or soy oil (or 50/50 salad and olive oil)

Place the mustard, salt and pepper, sugar, lemon juice, lemon rind and yolks in a blender and blend to mix. With the motor running add the oil slowly in a thin stream until it is fully incorporated and the mayonnaise is very thick. Makes 2½ cups. Keep refrigerated. Mayonnaise can be thinned with hot water.

Warm Salads

Warm salads make a good offering at any time, but especially over the colder months. The contrast of crisp cool salad ingredients with warm, juicy chicken or meat is very appealing.

Warm Chicken Liver Salad

Preparation Time: 10 minutes
Cooking Time: 6–7 minutes

¼ cup olive oil
3 rashers bacon, cut into small pieces
500g fresh chicken livers, membranes removed
1 big bunch fresh spinach or watercress, washed and broken into bite-sized pieces
2 tbsp extra virgin olive oil
salt and black pepper
2 tbsp spiced vinegar
1 tsp brown sugar
1 tsp smooth french mustard
3 tbsp water
Garnish: 1 orange or pear, cored and cut into segments

Heat the first measure of oil in a large frypan and cook bacon for a couple of minutes over high heat. Add the chicken livers and cook over high heat for 3–4 minutes until well browned but still pink in the centre. Toss the spinach leaves in the second measure of olive oil and season lightly with salt and pepper. Pile onto a shallow serving platter. Lift the bacon and chicken livers out of the cooking oil and arrange over the greens. Add the vinegar, sugar, mustard and water to the pan and stir until well combined. Pour over the salad. Garnish with wedges of orange or pear. Serves 4.

Salad of Garlic Prawns, Avocado and Beans

Prepare this tasty salad using chicken or squid in place of the prawns. Take care not to overcook the prawns.

Preparation Time: 15 minutes
Cooking Time: 5–6 minutes

about 20 large raw prawns, peeled and de-veined
1 tsp crushed garlic
3 tbsp olive oil
finely grated rind of 1 lemon
salt and white pepper to taste
2 tbsp lemon juice

Salad

6 large handfuls of mixed salad greens eg mixed lettuces, spinach leaves, lambs lettuce, chinese salad greens, etc, washed and dried
1 bunch watercress or arugula, leaves washed and dried
1 large firm but ripe avocado, cut in large dice
150–200g green beans, blanched
2 tbsp olive oil

Mix the prawns with the garlic and lemon rind. Heat the oil and stir fry the prawns over high heat for 2–3 minutes until they change colour. Remove from the heat, season to taste with salt and pepper, mix in lemon juice and reserve while assembling salad. Combine the salad greens with the avocado, beans, and olive oil and arrange on a large flat platter. Spoon over prawns and their dressing and serve. Serves 6 as an entree or 4 as a main course.

Winter Salad with Hot Bacon and Mushrooms

Preparation Time: 15 minutes
Cooking Time: 5 minutes

1 large bunch spinach, washed
1 big handful of watercress or endive
4 rashers bacon, cut into medium pieces
300g mushrooms, sliced thickly
3 tbsp olive oil
6 eggs, lightly poached
125g bleu de bresse or Kahurangi cheese
optional: bagel crisps or toasted almonds

Dressing

1 heaped tsp smooth fresh mustard
1 tsp brown sugar
2 tbsp tarragon vinegar
3 tbsp light olive oil
salt and freshly ground pepper
1 large egg yolk

Wash and dry the salad greens and lightly poach the eggs. Reserve aside, leaving the eggs in their pan for a quick reheating at serving time. In a pan cook the bacon and mushrooms over a low heat until the bacon is crisp and the mushrooms are dry. Combine the dressing ingredients together in a jar. Just prior to serving toss the salad greens in the dressing and arrange onto 6 plates. Divide wedges of cheese and optional croutons or nuts between the plates. Reheat the bacon mixture and the eggs. Sprinkle hot bacon and mushrooms over salad, along with any oil from cooking. Top each salad with a warm poached egg. Serves 6.

Warm Chicken Salad with Chilli Peanut Dressing

Preparation Time: 15 minutes
Cooking Time: 8 minutes

Salad

2 single skinless, boneless chicken breasts or 4
   skinless, boneless chicken thighs
1 tsp crushed garlic
1 tbsp lemon juice
2 tbsp salad or cooking oil
salt and pepper to season
1 lettuce, finely shredded and mixed with 2 tbsp
   lemon juice
3 spring onions, finely sliced
2 cups bean sprouts
1 red pepper, thinly sliced
3 tbsp fresh chopped mint
¼ cup chopped roasted peanuts

Dressing

2 tbsp crunchy peanut butter
2 tbsp hot chilli sauce
2 tsp fish sauce
6 tbsp hot water
2 tbsp lemon juice
garnish — ½ cup toasted peanuts, chopped, ¼ cup
   chopped coriander, basil or mint

Combine the chicken, garlic and lemon juice and leave to stand for 10 minutes while preparing the other ingredients. Heat the oil in a wok or large frypan. Season the chicken with salt and pepper and cook quickly. Remove and set aside to cool.

Arrange lettuce on a large platter, top with spring onions, sprouts, red pepper, mint and peanuts. Combine the dressing ingredients and spoon over. Slice cooked chicken and arrange over the top. Sprinkle with chopped peanuts and coriander. Serves 4.

Venison Salad with Watercress and Wild Berry Dressing

Preparation Time: 15 minutes
Cooking Time: 4 minutes

Farm-raised Cervena venison is wonderfully tender. Only qualified packhouses are licensed to use the Cervena appellation, through following stringent quality assurance procedures.

Winter Salad with Hot Bacon and Mushrooms
Warm Chicken Liver Salad

4×2cm-thick Cervena venison steaks
freshly ground black pepper
about 1 tbsp olive oil to cook steaks
1 large bunch watercress, washed and thick stems
   removed
2 oranges, peeled and segmented
½ cup fresh walnut halves
optional: ½ punnet blackberries or raspberries

Dressing

½ cup fresh or frozen berries
¼ cup light olive oil
2 tsp crushed garlic
½ cup orange juice
1 tbsp lemon juice
salt, pepper and a pinch of sugar

Season the venison well all over with pepper. Heat a little oil in a heavy pan and fry steaks for about 2 minutes each side, taking care not to overcook. Remove and allow to cool while preparing rest of salad. Puree the dressing ingredients together and toss three-quarters through the watercress. Arrange the greens on a large flat platter, scatter over the orange segments, nuts and optional berries. Slice the venison steaks thinly across the grain into 4–5 slices. Fan over the top of the salad. Spoon over the rest of the dressing. Serves 4.

Pasta and Rice

Nutritious, quick to cook and amazingly versatile, pasta is one of the mainstays of the 90's diet. It's hard to imagine that just a few years ago we hardly ate pasta.
There are still a lot of misconceptions about pasta being fattening. Pasta itself is not fattening, but it will be if you use cream or butter sauces with it. The recipes in this chapter feature some smart saucery using fresh vegetables, small amounts of lean proteins and, apart from the occasional indulgence, little in the way of fats.

Duck and Mushroom Fettuccine; Pasta with Eggplant, Spicy Sausage and Peppers; Spaghetti with Artichokes, Olives, Tomatoes and Pesto.

Pasta with Eggplant, Spicy Sausage and Peppers

You can imagine yourself on the Italian Riviera eating this rustic pasta dish. Full of earthy flavours, this easy sauce is scrumptious with pasta.

Preparation Time: 10 minutes
Cooking Time: 15 minutes

400g spaghetti
3 tbsp olive oil
2 tsp crushed garlic
2 medium eggplants, cut in chunks
1 large red pepper, seeds and pith removed, flesh diced
3–4 spicy sausages, eg Julia Colbasse, thinly sliced
2 tbsp tapenade
1 tsp crushed dry rosemary
2–3 tomatoes, chopped
200g green beans, blanched
salt and pepper to season
optional garnish: wilted spinach or rocket

Cook the pasta according to manufacturer's instructions. Heat the oil in a large pan and cook the garlic for 30 seconds. Add the eggplant, pepper, sausage, tapenade and rosemary, stirring frequently for 4–5 minutes. Mix in the tomatoes and beans and cook until the tomatoes are just softened. Season to taste. Prepare optional garnish by heating a little olive oil and gently frying spinach or rocket leaves until just wilted. Drain the pasta, toss through sauce, top with optional garnish and serve at once. Serves 4–5.

Variation: use pesto in place of tapenade.

Duck and Mushroom Fettuccine

This fantastic pasta dish is a quick assembly using a cooked duck (or chicken), fresh and dried mushrooms and good stock. Commercially made venison stock works extremely well (see page 9 for supplier). Ready-cooked duck can be purchased from Chinese food markets. If it is not available, substitute the flesh of a roasted chicken.

Preparation Time: 15 minutes plus soaking
Cooking Time: 10 minutes

5–6 dried mushrooms, soaked in ½ cup port or red wine
500g dried fettuccine
2 tbsp olive oil
2 tsp crushed garlic
300–400g field mushrooms, sliced
2 cups good beef or venison stock
pinch 5-spice powder
1 tsp cornflour mixed with a little water
shredded flesh of 1 cooked duck, minus bones, fat and skin
salt and black pepper
optional garnish: wilted watercress or spinach, crisp duck skin

Soak the mushrooms in the port until pliable. (Crisp the duck skin in a microwave or pan to use in a salad or as garnish for the pasta.) Cook the pasta according to manufacturer's instructions. (If preparing dish in advance, drain cooked pasta, cool under cold running water, drain thoroughly and mix through a little olive oil, to coat.) To make the sauce, heat the oil and cook the garlic for a few seconds. Add the field mushrooms and cook until dry. Slice the soaked mushrooms, and add to the pan with their liquid, stock and 5-spice. Simmer for 5 minutes. Thicken with the cornflour paste. Mix in the duck just before serving and adjust seasonings to taste. Pile the pasta onto a platter. Spoon over the sauce. For the garnish toss washed spinach or watercress leaves in a little olive oil to wilt. Serves 6.

Leek and Bacon Penne

Tossed Pastas
(Tomato Free)

People often think you have to make a wet sauce for pasta, but some of the nicest pastas are simply dressed with virgin olive oil or a pesto with a quickly sauteed mixture tossed through.

Leek and Bacon Penne

A quick, satisfying full-flavoured main course or entree. I sometimes add chicken for more variety.

Preparation Time: 10 minutes
Cooking Time: 15 minutes

400g penne pasta or other pasta shapes
2 tbsp butter
3–4 rashers bacon, diced
1 tsp crushed garlic
2 leeks, finely sliced
¾ cup white wine
¼ cup grated parmesan cheese
2–3 tbsp winter pesto (see page 9) or ¼ cup finely chopped parsley
½ cup sour cream (or ½ cup cream and 1 tbsp lemon juice)
optional: 1 avocado, diced
salt and freshly ground black pepper

Cook the pasta according to manufacturer's instructions. Melt the butter in a frypan. Add the bacon and cook until it is beginning to colour. Stir in the garlic and cook for 30 seconds. Add the leeks and wine, cover and cook gently until tender. Add the parmesan cheese, pesto or parsley, sour cream or cream and optional avocado. Season well with salt and plenty of pepper. Toss through the drained pasta and serve immediately. Serves 4–5.

Pasta with Pumpkin, Roasted Walnuts and Pesto

A simple, full-flavoured pasta that is put together in minutes. Here it stands as a vegetarian dish, but it can easily be extended with a pan-fried chicken breast sliced over the top.

Preparation Time: 5 minutes
Cooking Time: 10–12 minutes

300g good-quality dried spaghetti, or 400g fresh linguine
¼ cup olive oil
1 cup shelled fresh walnuts
600g pumpkin, peeled and diced into cubes (or buy ready chopped)
½ cup winter parsley pesto (see page 9 for recipe)
optional: 100g fresh mozzarella, cut in cubes

Cook the pasta according to manufacturer's instructions. While it cooks, heat the oil and gently fry the walnuts until they turn pale gold. Lift from pan and reserve, saving the oil in the pan. Add the pumpkin, cover pan and cook over medium-low heat for about 6–8 minutes until tender (or microwave for 5 minutes, then drain, add to pan and toss in oil to coat). Drain the pasta, toss in pumpkin, walnuts, pesto and optional mozzarella. Serve immediately. Serves 4.

Pasta with Spinach and Feta

Pasta with Spinach and Feta

This simple fresh pasta is a weekly staple in our household. Use a good quality olive oil.

Preparation Time: 10 minutes
Cooking Time: 15 minutes

400g dried Italian pasta (spirals, penne or shells)
2 tbsp olive oil
1 large onion, finely diced
2 tsp crushed garlic
1 large bunch spinach, washed, stalks removed and
*   finely chopped*
200g feta cheese, crumbled
freshly ground black pepper to taste
good pinch nutmeg

Cook the pasta according to manufacturer's instructions. While the pasta cooks, prepare the sauce. Heat the oil in a pan and cook the onion until soft. Add the garlic and sizzle for a few seconds. Add the spinach to the pan and cook a further minute. Add the feta and season with pepper and nutmeg. Toss through the cooked pasta. Sprinkle with plenty of freshly ground black pepper and serve immediately. Serves 4.

Pasta with Bacon, Avocado and Mushrooms

Homemade mayonnaise makes a great sauce for simple pastas and sautes. It needs to be added at the end so the egg doesn't separate.

Preparation Time: 10 minutes
Cooking Time: 10–12 minutes

400g pasta shapes, preferably spirals or bows
1 tbsp butter
3 rashers bacon, finely diced
300g mushrooms, thinly sliced
1 tsp crushed garlic

½ cup fresh chopped herbs, eg basil, tarragon,
*   oregano, parsley*
½ cup fresh homemade mayonnaise (see page 39)
1 tbsp lemon juice
1–2 firm avocados, peeled and diced
garnish: grated parmesan cheese

Cook the pasta according to manufacturer's instructions. While the pasta cooks, prepare the sauce. Melt the butter in a heavy pan and cook the bacon until it starts to brown. Add the mushrooms and garlic and cook until the pan is dry. Stir in the herbs. Drain the cooked pasta, combine the mayonnaise and lemon juice and toss through the cooked pasta. Add the mushroom mixture and avocado and toss to combine. Garnish with the parmesan cheese. Serves 4.

Penne with Feta, Olives, Rosemary and Chillies

Another good store cupboard pasta. Lightly cooked vegetables, such as spinach, beans or zucchini, are a good addition.

Preparation Time: 5 minutes
Cooking Time: 10–12 minutes

500g dried Italian penne pasta (or other pasta
*   shapes)*
¼ cup extra virgin olive oil
¾ cup black Calamata olives
1 tbsp fresh chopped rosemary or 1 tsp dried rosemary
1 dried chilli, finely chopped
salt and freshly ground pepper
optional: ¼ cup sundried tomatoes, roughly chopped
250g feta or chevre salade cheese, crumbled

Cook the pasta according to manufacturer's instructions. Heat the oil with all the other ingredients, except the cheese. Toss the olive mixture and the cheese through the cooked pasta. Serve immediately. Serves 5–6.

Chilli Mussel Fettuccine

With A Bottle Of Pasta Sauce

Bottled pasta sauce is a marvellous standby for impromptu meals.
The quality of most brands is so good that it's hardly worth making your
own. Most people have a repertoire of pasta dishes they make using bottled
pasta sauce as a base. Here are some of our favourites.

Pasta with Country Chicken Sauce

The chicken in this recipe simmers gently in the prepared sauce, emerging moist, tender and lightly perfumed with the sauce flavourings.

Preparation Time: 5 minutes
Cooking Time: 15 minutes

400g–500g fettuccine
1 tbsp oil
1 tsp crushed garlic
½ cup white wine
2 cups prepared pasta sauce
salt, freshly ground black pepper and a pinch of
* sugar*
1 tsp each oregano and chilli sauce
400g lean, skinless, boneless raw chicken (thighs,
* diced*

Cook the pasta according to manufacturer's instructions. While the pasta is cooking make the sauce. Heat the oil in a large pan and sizzle the garlic for a few seconds. Add the wine, pasta sauce and seasonings. Bring to a simmer. Add the chicken, cover and simmer for 10–15 minutes until the chicken is cooked. Serve over cooked, drained pasta. Serves 4–5.

Chilli Mussel Fettuccine

Smoked mussels add an intense flavour and richness to this easy pasta dish — great for a midweek dinner on the run.

Preparation Time: 5 minutes
Cooking Time: 5–10 minutes

400g fettuccine
1 tbsp oil
1 tsp crushed garlic
2 cups prepared pasta sauce
200g smoked or chilli mussels, sliced
1 tbsp sweet chilli sauce
salt and pepper and a pinch of sugar
optional: 2–3 tbsp pesto
optional garnish: diced green pepper and finely
* sliced spring onions*

Cook the fettuccine according to manufacturer's instructions. Heat the oil in a frypan and cook the garlic for 30 seconds. Add the pasta sauce, mussels, chilli sauce and seasonings. Simmer for 5 minutes. Mix in the pesto. Toss the sauce through the cooked pasta, garnish and serve immediately. Serves 4–5.

Pasta Vongole

Pasta Vongole
(with Cockles and Tomato Pesto Sauce)

Fresh shellfish, prepared pasta sauce and pesto create a light fresh pasta sauce.

Preparation Time: 5 minutes
Cooking Time: 12–15 minutes

400g pasta spirals or shells
1.5kg live cockles (or mussels)
2 tbsp lemon juice or white wine
2 cups prepared pasta sauce
2 tbsp herb pesto

Cook the pasta according to manufacturer's instructions. Place the shellfish in a pot with the lemon juice or wine, cover and cook, removing as they open. (Cockles open very quickly, so keep a close watch on them so they don't overcook.) Add the pasta sauce and pesto to the juices in the pot and heat. Remove the top shell from each cockle. Return the cockles to the pot to heat through. Pile the cooked pasta into a serving bowl and pour over the sauce. Serves 4.

Speedy Pasta Combos

Spaghetti with Artichokes, Olives, Tomatoes and Pesto

A well stocked store cupboard allows for the quick creation of a variety of pasta dishes. When the fridge is bare this recipe makes a great standby.

Preparation Time: 5 minutes
Cooking Time: 5 minutes

400–500g dried spaghetti
3 tbsp olive oil
2 tsp minced garlic
400g tin artichokes, drained and chopped
½ cup black olives, halved
400g tin tomatoes in brine, drained and chopped
¼ cup herb pesto (see page 9 for recipe)
optional: 5–6 sundried tomatoes

Cook the pasta according to manufacturer's instructions. While it cooks, heat the oil in a large pan and cook the garlic for a few seconds . Add all the other ingredients, except the pasta and pesto and toss to combine and heat through. Mix pesto through the cooked drained pasta. Toss in the sauce. Serves 4–5.

Spaghetti with Smoked Salmon and Green Peppercorns

The ultimate store cupboard dinner for the gourmet, this next recipe is our favourite holiday treat.

Preparation Time: 5 minutes
Cooking Time 10 minutes

500g dried spaghetti
100g butter, melted
¼ cup lime or lemon juice
3 tbsp chopped green peppercorns
⅓ side sliced smoked salmon, diced (about 250–300g)

Cook the spaghetti according to manufacturer's instructions. Heat the butter until melted, then mix through the lime or lemon juice and peppercorns. Toss through the drained pasta and salmon. Serve immediately. Serves 5–6.

Other Speedy Pasta Combinations:

• Artichokes, olives, tomatoes and pesto
• Spinach, mozzarella and pesto

Decadence In Cream Sauces

Cream makes a fantastic base for a pasta sauce, albeit a trifle rich.
If including cream in your menu, keep it to a single course. If it's in
the dessert, don't use it in the main and vice versa, otherwise your menu
will be too heavy.
For the simplest creamy pasta dishes heat the cream, allowing about 250–300ml
per 400g dried pasta, simmering until it reduces to just coat the back of a spoon.
Add flavours of your choice, eg garlic, parmesan or pesto. Cooked bacon,
chicken, broccoli, mushrooms, nuts, etc can be incorporated as desired.
The flavour-carrying properties of cream form the medium that
links all the elements.

Creamy Pasta with Bacon, Chicken, Hazelnuts and Beans

This substantial pasta dish makes great buffet fare. It could be put into a casserole or baking dish and finished in the oven.

Preparation Time: 10 minutes
Cooking Time: 15 minutes

400g beans, sliced (or use frozen)
400g pasta spirals or tubes
1 tbsp oil
3 rashers bacon, finely diced
200g skinless, boneless chicken, thinly sliced
1 tsp crushed garlic
200ml cream
½ cup grated parmesan cheese
salt and plenty of freshly ground black pepper
½ cup roasted hazelnuts

Blanch the beans in boiling water for 1 minute. Drain and refresh in cold water. Cook the pasta according to manufacturer's instructions. To prepare the sauce, heat the oil and fry the bacon and chicken until the chicken is just cooked and the bacon is starting to crisp. Add the garlic and allow to sizzle for a few seconds. Add the cream and half the parmesan cheese and simmer 2–3 minutes. Add the beans to heat through. Toss the sauce through the pasta, seasoning well with freshly ground black pepper and a little salt. Mix in the hazelnuts and remaining cheese. Transfer to a serving dish and serve immediately. Serves 4.

Fettuccine with Ham, Broccoli and Pine Nuts

Broccoli lightens and freshens creamy tasty pasta.

Preparation Time: 10 minutes
Cooking Time: 12–15 minutes

Creamy Pasta with Bacon, Chicken, Hazelnuts and Beans

1 head broccoli, cut into florets
400g fresh fettuccine noodles or dried pasta
200g ham, diced 1cm cubes
2 tsp crushed garlic
2 tsp butter
300ml cream
6 tbsp grated parmesan cheese
1–2 tsp lemon juice
salt and freshly ground black pepper to taste
½ cup toasted pine nuts
¼ cup finely chopped parsley or 2–3 tbsp herb pesto

Blanch the broccoli florets in boiling water for 2 minutes. Drain and cool in cold water. Reserve. Cook the pasta according to manufacturer's instructions. Place the ham, garlic and butter in a frypan and cook for 2 minutes. Add the cream and simmer until the sauce just coats the back of a spoon. Mix in the parmesan cheese, broccoli and lemon juice. Season with salt and pepper. Just before serving, mix through the pine nuts and parsley. Toss sauce through cooked, drained pasta. Serves 4–5.

Variation: add 2–3 tbsp sundried tomato pesto in with the cream.

Creamy Pasta and Scallops

This heavenly pasta makes great fare for a dinner party or romantic meal. The sauce and pasta can be prepared ahead of time and reheated. Cook the scallops just before serving. Oysters and even diced fresh fish are also superb this way — cook the same way as the scallops.

Preparation Time: 5 minutes
Cooking Time: 10 minutes

¼ cup finely chopped shallots
2 tbsp butter
1 tsp tomato paste
1 cup dry white wine
300ml cream
600–800g fresh fettuccine or tagliolini
30–50 fresh scallops, cleaned
¼ cup chopped chervil, dill or parsley
salt and black pepper
garnish: fine dice of red pepper

In a large heavy pan cook the shallots in the butter until tender but not browned. Add the tomato paste and cook a few seconds. Add the wine and bring to a fast boil. Mix in the cream. Boil until the sauce has a light coating consistency (sauce can be prepared ahead to this point).

Cook the pasta according to manufacturer's instructions and warm the pasta bowls. When the pasta is nearly cooked, add the scallops to the hot sauce, cover and cook on lowest possible heat for about 2 minutes, stirring to ensure even cooking. Do not overcook. Mix in the herbs and season to taste. Divide the cooked pasta between heated pasta bowls and spoon over sauce. Garnish with red pepper. Serves 6–8.

Menu

Sunday Lunch

Caesar Salad

Creamy Pasta with Bacon, Chicken, Hazelnuts and Beans

Greek Orange Syrup Cake and Whipped Cream

Preparation
1 Prepare salad greens, dressing and croutons.
2 Make sauce for pasta.
3 Cook pasta, cool under cold water, drain thoroughly, add oil and cover.
4 Make cake, slice oranges and drizzle with a little honey.

Serving
1 Assemble salad.
2 Reheat pasta and sauce and combine.
3 Garnish cake.

Suggested Wine
Riesling or Chardonnay

Pasta with cream and . . .

- Salmon, capers and lemon juice
- Pesto, ham and asparagus
- Bacon, peas and mint
- Pesto, chicken and broccoli
- Sundried tomato pesto, shrimps and wilted watercress
- Anchovies, green olives, garlic and grated parmesan cheese

Risotto — Quiche Of The 90s

In the 80s we all made quiche. In the 90s it's risotto — a thoroughly versatile, satisfying and nutritious staple that can be made from scratch in less than 30 minutes. Italian risotto rice has a unique structure, releasing starch to give creaminess while retaining an excellent texture. Its disadvantage is that generally you have to stand over the stove and stir for the entire 20 minutes it takes the rice to cook. Vialone Nano and Carnaroli rices, both sold under the Ferron brand, are worth looking out for, as they are unique varieties of risotto rices that do not require constant stirring. They have an excellent texture and attractive nutty flavour.

Risotto can be semi-cooked in advance for a dinner party. Simmer the rice with half the broth for 10 minutes until it has absorbed all the liquid. Turn onto a tray and cool quickly. When ready to serve, add the rest of the boiling stock and simmer with other flavourings for 7–8 minutes until the rice is cooked and creamy.

Mushroom Risotto

Vegetarians may prefer to use a vegetable stock. The flavour won't be as dense, so try adding 2 teaspoons of crushed garlic.

Preparation Time: 10 minutes plus soaking
Cooking Time: 25 minutes

50g dried porcini mushrooms or dried Chinese
  mushrooms
½ cup port or red wine to soak
50g butter
1 onion, finely diced
400g field mushrooms, thinly sliced
white pepper
about 2 tbsp extra virgin olive oil
2½ cups Vialone Nano or other shortgrain Italian
  rice, eg Arborio
1 glass dry white wine
about 5 cups good beef, venison or chicken stock,
  boiling
½ cup grated parmesan cheese
2 tbsp chopped parsley

Soak the porcini in the port for about 1 hour. Strain, retaining the liquid and slice finely. In a pan, melt the butter and cook the onion until soft. Add the field mushrooms and pepper and cook until dry. Reserve. In a heavy pot heat the olive oil and toast the rice for 2–3 minutes until coated and warmed through. Add the wine, boiling stock, cooked mushrooms, soaked mushrooms and their liquid and cover. Lower the heat and simmer approximately 20 minutes, stirring occasionally. Before serving, add the parmesan cheese and parsley and stir gently. Serves 4–5.

Variation: *Duck Risotto*
Add the flesh of 1 cooked duck to the risotto just before serving. Garnish with crisped duck skin and parmesan.

Pumpkin Risotto

Preparation Time: 10 minutes
Cooking Time: 20 minutes

2 tsp crushed garlic
1 onion, finely chopped
¼ cup extra virgin olive oil
1 medium pumpkin, peeled and cut in small pieces
salt and freshly ground black pepper
1 glass semi-dry red wine
2 cups Vialone Nano or other shortgrain Italian rice
about 4 cups good beef or venison broth, boiling
2 tbsp butter

Duck Risotto; Pumpkin Risotto

¼ cup chopped parsley or coriander
½ cup grated parmesan cheese
optional: dash of lemon rind
200g mushrooms, sliced and fried in butter until soft

Place the garlic and the onion into a heavy-bottomed saucepan over a medium heat with half the olive oil. Add the pumpkin and salt and pepper, stir and cook for 2 minutes. Add the wine and cover. Cook the pumpkin until it starts to soften, but still remains in pieces. In another heavy-bottomed pan, heat the remaining olive oil and toast the rice, stirring for 2–3 minutes. Add the boiling broth, cover and cook for 18 minutes, stirring occasionally. Once the rice has absorbed all the liquid add the cooked pumpkin, butter, parsley or coriander, parmesan cheese and optional lemon rind and mushrooms. Stand covered for 5 minutes before serving. Serves 4.

NB: If using arborio rice for any risotto, add the boiling stock gradually, ladling it over the rice to just cover at all times. Stir frequently.

51

Fast Fish

*For an island nation, with
commercial harvests of more than 75
different seafood species, we are
exceptionally unadventurous seafood
eaters. Most of us have a handful of
seafood varieties that we like to eat,
but tend to avoid others because we
don't know what to do with them.
Apart from being an excellent source
of low-fat protein and minerals, seafood is also quick to cook. Fish varies
considerably in texture from species to
species, so choose a cooking method
that will suit the variety — butterfish,
for example, is no good for stir-frying,
as its fine flake causes it to fall apart
if stirred during cooking.
The recipes on these next pages are
designed to assist you to be a more
adventurous seafood eater. Buy
seafoods really fresh and take great
care not to overcook them — you
really can't go wrong.*

Mediterranean Skewered Fish and Vegetables; Flash-
roasted Fish with Pesto on a Bed of Ribbon Zucchini;
Gurnard with Indian Spices on a Bed of Sesame
Coriander Noodles

53

Gurnard with Indian Spices

You need thick fish fillets for this dish. Choose a well-flavoured species, such as gurnard, that won't be over-powered by the spicy marinade.

Preparation Time: 5 minutes plus marinating
Cooking Time: 6–8 minutes

¼ cup lemon juice
1 tsp salt
1 tsp black pepper
1 tbsp garlic, crushed
4 boneless fish fillets (at least 1.5cm thick)
½ cup cream
1 tsp prepared mustard
1 tsp garam masala
garnish: chopped fresh coriander or fresh shreds of
    cucumber rind

Combine the lemon juice, salt, pepper and garlic and mix through the fish. Leave to marinate for 30 minutes. Combine the cream, mustard and garam masala and add to the fish, mixing well. (At this stage the fish can be marinated in the fridge for a further hour if desired.) Preheat the oven to 250°C. Place the fish on a baking tray, spoon over extra marinade and bake for 6–8 minutes until fish shows no resistance when pressed. Garnish with sauce, coriander or fine shreds of cucumber rind. Serves 4.

Flash-roasted Fish with Pesto

Salmon, hapuku, monkfish, blue nose or any other moist, dense fish will respond well to this easy treatment. The key is in choosing thick fillets and not over-cooking. This is a good recipe for a crowd — allow 1 fillet of fish, 1 tbsp pesto and a few strips of roasted red pepper per serve.

Preparation Time: 5 minutes
Cooking Time: 6–8 minutes

4 × 180–200g fresh boneless fish pieces or fillets,
    eg salmon, bluenose, hapuku, ling
salt and freshly ground black pepper, to season
about ¼ cup herb pesto
garnish: strips of roasted red pepper

Preheat the oven to 250°C. Place the fillets in a lightly oiled baking dish and fold under any shallow ends. Season lightly with salt and pepper. Bake for 6–8 minutes until the fish shows no resistance when pressed. Do not overcook — the fish should still be slightly translucent in the centre. Transfer to heated serving plates. Spoon on a dollop of pesto and garnish with strips of red pepper. Serves 4.

Oriental Barbecue Tuna Steaks

Tuna, kingfish and other 'game fish' require very quick cooking as they easily become dry. The dense texture and flavour of game fish make it ideal for marinating.

Preparation Time: 5 minutes plus marinating
Cooking Time: 2 minutes

6 fresh tuna steaks, approx 1.5cm thickness
2 tbsp soy sauce
2 tsp finely chopped fresh root ginger
2 tbsp sesame oil (or plain oil)
juice of 1 juicy lemon

Combine the steaks with all other ingredients and leave to marinate in the fridge for at least 1 hour (or up to 4 hours). Preheat a heavy pan or barbecue and oil lightly. Drain off the marinade and barbecue or pan-fry steaks over high heat for about 40 seconds per side, until just firm. Do not overcook — the flesh should be slightly translucent in the centre. Serves 6.

Mediterranean Skewered Fish and Vegetables

Assemble these terrific kebabs in the afternoon ready for a barbecue or summer dinner on the lawn.

Preparation Time: 10 minutes plus
    30 minutes soaking skewers
Cooking Time: 4–5 minutes

4 thick fillets boneless, medium or firm textured
    white fish, eg hapuku, blue nose, snapper
1 small eggplant, sliced thickly
2–3 tbsp olive oil
½ red pepper, cut into 2cm dice
1 lemon, sliced thinly
2 tbsp herb pesto mixed with 2 tbsp olive oil
freshly ground black pepper
8 skewers soaked in water for 30 minutes

Cut the fish into 3cm dice. Halve the eggplant slices and fry in the first measure of oil until softened. Thread all the ingredients alternately onto skewers. Chill until ready to cook. Combine pesto and oil with black pepper. Brush over kebabs. Grill or barbecue for 4–5 minutes or until cooked through.

Bamboo skewers require soaking for about 30 minutes in cold water before using or else they will char. Bamboo skewers are also useful for holding together chicken cavities and meat rolls.

Florentine Fish Rolls

Flat fish species, such as sole, flounder and john dory, are ideal for rolling, as they have thin fillets. Other species, such as orange roughy, creamfish, salmon and skate, can also be used if you choose thin fillets.

Preparation Time: 20 minutes
Cooking Time: 3–4 minutes

3 tbsp butter
1 tsp crushed garlic
2 tbsp parsley, finely chopped
4 boneless skinned thin fish fillets, eg john dory,
*   orange roughy or sole, halved lengthwise*
8 large spinach leaves, blanched and well dried
juice of 1 lemon

Mix the butter, garlic and parsley to form a paste. Spread about 1 tablespoon over each fillet. Roll up each piece of fish tightly then wrap with spinach leaves. Space evenly in a microwave dish and cover with plastic wrap. Microwave on high for 3–4 minutes. Test with a skewer — there should not be any resistance if fish is cooked. Spoon over the pan juices, and lemon juice and serve. Serves 4.

To cook conventionally: cover the fish rolls and bake at 180°C for about 15 minutes until fish is cooked through.

Florentine Fish Rolls

bake at 180°C for 15–20 minutes. Uncover, combine the topping ingredients and sprinkle over the fish rolls. Place under a preheated grill for 2–3 minutes until brown and crunchy. Serves 4.

Caribbean Fish Rolls

Bananas and fish are a wonderful combination. Adapt this recipe in other ethnic tangents — add coriander and lime juice for an Asian-style fish roll, or ground cumin, chilli and cheese for a Mexican interpretation.

Preparation Time: 10 minutes
Cooking Time: 7 minutes

4 flat fish fillets, eg john dory, orange roughy, sole
2 bananas, sliced diagonally
¼ cup grated cheese
freshly ground black pepper
toothpicks

Crumble Topping

½ cup wholemeal bread crumbs
3 tbsp parmesan cheese
¼ tsp paprika

Cut the fish fillets in half lengthwise to give 2 long strips each. Divide the banana and cheese on top of the fillets. Sprinkle with freshly ground pepper and roll up. Secure each roll with a toothpick. Place in a microwave dish. Cover and microwave on 80% power for 4 minutes or

Menu

A Mid-Week Business Dinner

Florentine Fish Rolls
Gourmet Rice
Sauteed Vegetables
Fresh Fruit Salad
with Elizabeth David's Cremets d'Angers

Preparation
1 Cook the rice.
2 Prepare fish rolls.
3 Prepare dessert and chill.
4 Prepare sauteed vegetables: slice a variety of vegetables, allowing 100–150g per person. Par cook by boiling for 1 minute or cooking in the microwave on 100% power for 2 minutes. When ready to serve cook the vegetables in a preheated frypan with 1 tbsp oil until lightly browned. Sprinkle with the juice of half a lemon and freshly ground black pepper.

Suggested Wine
Sauvignon Blanc

Quick Treatments
with Flavoured Butters

Flavoured butters and oils are complementary to seafood without overpowering its delicate taste. This is a good way to elevate the simplest fish cooking techniques, such as pan-frying and grilling. The end result should not see pools of butter in the bottom of the plate — about 1–2 teaspoons of flavoured butter per portion will be sufficient. Flavoured butters will keep in the fridge for about 7–10 days.

Sesame Ginger Butter

(pictured on crayfish, on right)

100g butter
¼ cup finely chopped root ginger
2 tsp sesame oil
1 finely chopped spring onion

Blend the butter, ginger, oil and spring onion. Makes enough for 6–8 servings of seafood. Store in the refrigerator.

Red Pepper Butter

flesh of 2 roasted peppers (see page 9 for technique)
1 tsp crushed garlic
1 tbsp butter
½ cup white wine
2 tbsp lemon juice
200g butter, softened

Roughly chop the roasted peppers. Cook the garlic in the first quantity of butter for a few seconds. Add the peppers, wine and lemon juice. Cook, stirring occasionally, until the pan is dry. Allow to cool, then place in a blender. Blend until the mixture forms a roughish paste, then blend in the butter until it is evenly incorporated. Makes enough for about 15 servings of seafood. Store in the refrigerator.

Green Peppercorn Butter

2 tbsp butter
½ tsp grated lemon rind
1 tbsp green peppercorns
1 tbsp lemon juice

Combine the butter with all the other ingredients. Makes enough for about 6 servings of seafood. Store in the refrigerator.

Garlic Pine Nut Butter

½ cup pine nuts
60g butter
1 small clove garlic, crushed
2 tbsp chopped parsley
1 tbsp lemon juice
pinch pepper

Microwave the nuts on a plate for about 2 minutes, shaking every 30 seconds until lightly golden, or toast in a pan. Allow to cool, then place in a blender with butter and all the other ingredients. Blend until semi smooth. Makes enough for 4–6 servings of seafood. Store in the refrigerator.

Scallops Cooked in the Shell
with Flavoured Butter

Serve scallops piled into cleaned scallop shells, and garnish with fresh herbs and a slice of lemon.
To barbecue scallops in the shell, clean fresh scallops and place in cleaned shells with about ½ tsp butter each, turning the scallops in the butter as it boils. Cook just until scallops change colour.

Crayfish with Flavoured Butter

1 fresh crayfish
1 quantity sesame ginger butter

Remove the raw crayfish tail from the body and cut in half lengthwise. Spread 2 tsp of ginger sesame butter over the flesh of each half. Preheat grill and cook the tails for 8–10 minutes. Serve with a fan of fresh mango. Serves 1–2. Recipe easily doubles or triples.

Crayfish with Sesame Ginger Butter

Grilled Fish Steaks with Flavoured Butter

Spread fish steaks or fillets with 1–2 tsp flavoured butter. Cook under a preheated grill for 3–4 minutes without turning until fish gives when pressed or a skewer inserted meets no resistance. Serve topped with an extra knob of flavoured butter if desired.

Barbecue Mussels and Pipis with Flavoured Butter

Cook shellfish on a heated barbecue plate until they start to open. Heat flavoured butter. Transfer the cooked shellfish to a bowl and drizzle over the flavoured butter.

Pan-fried Scallops or Fish Fillets with Flavoured Butter

Heat the flavoured butter of your choice in a pan, allowing about 2 tsp per serving. Cook scallops or fingers of boneless fresh fish in hot butter over medium-high heat for 2–3 minutes until just cooked. Serve at once.

> If you want any shellfish opened without cooking them or having to shuck them, simply freeze in a single layer for about 1 hour. They will pop open, making it very easy to remove the top shell.

Fish Steaks with Sundried Tomatoes and Peppers

Sundried tomatoes add an intense summer flavour to any dish. Here they form a light topping that contrasts nicely with the dense taste of the fish.

Preparation Time: 5 minutes plus marinating
Cooking Time: 5–6 minutes

2 tbsp oil or melted butter
1 tsp freshly ground black pepper
¼ tsp salt
optional: pinch of chilli powder
2 sundried tomatoes in oil, finely diced
¼ red pepper, finely diced
*4 medium to firm textured fish steaks, e.g. hapuku,
   kingfish, lemon fish*

Combine the oil, pepper, salt, optional chilli powder, sundried tomatoes and red pepper and smear over either side of the fish steaks. Leave for at least 10 minutes or up to 4 hours in the fridge. Grill for 5–6 minutes, until the steaks are cooked through. Accompany with Mexican tomato salsa (see page 64), oven fries and a salad. Serves 4.

Fish Fillets with Toasted Almonds and Lime Juice

Any type of toasted nut goes well with fresh fish. Adding lemon or lime juice offsets the richness of the fish.

Preparation Time: 5 minutes
Cooking Time: 6 minutes

2 tbsp butter
½ cup flaked almonds
*2 fresh firm boneless fish fillets of any type, except
   game fish*
juice of 1 large lime or lemon

Melt the butter, then add the almonds and mix to coat. Cook for 2–3 minutes, either in the microwave or in a pan, stirring every 30–40 seconds until lightly golden. Place fish in a shallow microwave dish, folding shallow edges under. Drain the butter from almonds and brush over the fish. Squeeze over lemon or lime juice. Cover tightly and microwave for 2 minutes until just cooked. Coat the top of each fillet with a layer of toasted almonds. Serves 2.

To cook conventionally: grill fish fillets, then top with almonds.

Mediterranean Squid

Squid is rendered wonderfully tender in this densely flavoured sauce. Commercially prepared pasta sauce and pesto cuts the preparation time to a minimum.

Preparation Time: 5 minutes
Cooking Time: 15 minutes

2 large squid tubes
2 tbsp oil
2 tsp crushed garlic
2 cups tomato pasta sauce
¼ cup white wine
salt and freshly ground black pepper to taste
*2–3 tbsp herb pesto, eg basil or parsley (see page
   9 for recipe)*
185g feta cheese
optional: ½ cup black olives

Slice the squid into very thin rings. Heat the oil in a large pan. Add the garlic and cook for 30 seconds. Stir in the pasta sauce and wine and simmer gently, uncovered, for 10 minutes or until the sauce is fairly thick. Add the squid to the tomato sauce and simmer for 2–3 minutes just until it turns opaque. Season to taste. Mix in the pesto and crumble over the cheese. Garnish with the optional olives and serve immediately. Serves 4–5. Accompany with rice.

Parmesan Grilled Fish

Parmesan Grilled Fish

Parmesan cheese makes a great coating for fish. If preferred the fish can be pan-fried rather than baked.

Preparation Time: 5 minutes
Cooking Time: 10–12 minutes

4 fresh boneless fish fillets of any type except gamefish
1 egg, lightly beaten
½ cup grated parmesan cheese
½ cup fresh breadcrumbs
1 tsp dried oregano

Preheat oven to 200°C. Dip fish into egg. Combine other ingredients and coat fish pieces. Place on a baking tray and bake for 10–12 minutes or until a skewer inserted into fish meets no resistance. Serves 4.

Filo as a Wrapper

Filo pastry makes a great wrapper for seafood. Form a stack of 5–6 layers of filo with melted butter or oil between each layer to give a good crunchy coating around the filling. Top the boneless fish with flavoured cream cheese mixtures, pesto or tapenade, or any of your favourite combinations. Fold the filo over the fish to encase in a parcel or purse shape. Brush with melted butter or oil and bake at 180°C. They will take about 20–25 minutes to cook.

Matching the Fish with the Method

Baking

Suitable for whole fish, fillets or steaks of 2cm or more thickness. A good method when cooking for a crowd.
Suitable Species — all types except gamefish, eg tuna and kingfish, which tend to dry out too much.

Flash-roasting

Ideal for whole fish and fish fillets or steaks. A very high temperature is required so the fish cooks quickly and does not dry out.
Suitable Species — all

Pan-frying

Suitable for boneless fillets and steaks, small whole fish and flat fish. For more delicate flaky species, such as butterfish, cook in a covered pan without turning.
Suitable Species — all

Grilling (in the oven)

Suitable for fish steaks or fillets less than 2cm thick to avoid drying out. The high heat of the grill can dry out the top surface of the fish, so you may wish to brush it with butter or oil before cooking. Cook the fish 6–10cm from the heat source without turning.
Suitable Species — medium to firm-textured fish, such as monkfish, mullet, gurnard, ling, piper, warehou and all gamefish.

Barbecuing

Excellent for fish steaks, whole fish and shellfish.
Suitable Species — game fish, plus other oily, firm-textured species, shellfish.

Steaming and Microwaving

Ideal for species with a delicate flavour plus all shellfish. The cooking vessel must be tightly covered.
Suitable Species — orange roughy, brill and other flat fish, eg blue cod, tarakihi, john dory, snapper, skate, butterfish

Stir-frying

Suitable for species with a large flake and firm texture. The Chinese coat their fish in cornflour before cooking to provide a protective coating that prevents fillets and pieces from falling apart during the stir-frying process.
Suitable Species — hapuku, monkfish, ling, tarakihi

Poaching

Cover the fish by 2cm with cold liquid and bring to a shimmer. Once the liquid reaches a shimmer, regardless of its size the fish will take 12 minutes to cook. The time remains the same because the water will only come to a shimmer when the internal temperature of the fish has reached a suitable heat.
Suitable Species — whole fish, eg gurnard

Thai Fish Curry

With a can of coconut cream, fish curries are one of the simplest, great-tasting one-pot dinners. You can use green curry paste, chilli powder or chilli sauce to provide the desired curry flavour — each will give quite a different effect. If desired, add a few curry leaves or a tablespoon of minced lemongrass to the sauce during cooking.

Preparation Time: 10 minutes
Cooking Time: 10 minutes

1 tbsp oil
1 large onion, finely diced

1 tsp each of crushed garlic and paprika
1–2 tbsp green curry paste or 1–2 tsp chilli paste or 1–2 tbsp hot chilli sauce (to taste)
400ml tin coconut cream
500g–600g boneless fresh fish, diced, eg bluenose, hapuku, ling, gurnard
salt and freshly ground black pepper to taste
2–3 tbsp finely chopped fresh coriander (or chopped parsley)

Heat the oil and cook the onion until soft. Add the garlic, paprika, curry paste or chilli and cook a further 30 seconds. Add the coconut cream and simmer 5 minutes. Mix in the fish, stirring well to distribute evenly in the sauce. Cook for 4–5 minutes until the fish is

Texture/Flavour

	Delicate	Medium	Full
Delicate	flounder/sole	butterfish	herring
	orange roughy	pink salmon	sardine
	skate	gemfish	eel
	hoki	(snake mackerel)	
	brill		
	hake		
	grenadiers		
	creamfish		
Medium	blue cod	red cod	anchovy
	snapper	hapuku	Atlantic salmon
	tarakihi	barracouta	mackerel
	john dory	piper	barracouta
		maumau	kahawai
		warehou	trevally
Dense	moki	shark	bluenose
	sea perch	ling	tuna
		gurnard	marlin
		kingfish	
		conger eel	
		monkfish	
		oreo dory	
		mullet	

How to Select and Store Fish

- When buying whole fish look for a clear eye and shiny scales. If the eye has sunken or is cloudy the fish isn't fresh. The gills should be red, if they are brown or pinkish the fish has started to deteriorate.

- When you press a whole fish it should feel springy and bouncy, otherwise it's not fresh. Fish fillets should feel springy and look translucent and shiny. Don't buy them if they look dull and limp.

- Fresh fish should smell of the sea, it should never have a fishy or strong smell.

- If buying frozen fish thaw it in the fridge to prevent water loss.

- Keep fish chilled at all times and eat as soon as possible after you have made the purchase. Every hour at room temperature equates to a days shelf life in the refrigerator.

- Don't eat shellfish that have died before you cook them. Discard any that won't close when you tap them or those that won't open after cooking.

just cooked. Avoid stirring towards the end of cooking, as the fish will break up. Garnish with coriander and serve. Accompany with rice. Serves 4.

Cockles or Mussels with Pesto Cream Sauce

This yummy sauce is also delicious with pan-fried fish — you can thicken it with a teaspoon of cornflour if desired.

Preparation Time: 15 minutes
Cooking Time: 10 minutes

1 tbsp butter
1 tsp crushed garlic
½ cup dry white wine
30–35 fresh cockles or 20–25 live mussels, scrubbed clean
1 cup cream
2 tbsp pesto (see page 9 for recipe)
freshly ground black pepper

In a large saucepan heat the butter and cook the garlic for 30 seconds. Add the wine and shellfish. Cover tightly and cook for 5–6 minutes, removing the shellfish as they open. Cover and keep warm. Add the cream to the saucepan liquids. Bring to a fast boil and simmer for 2–3 minutes. Mix in the pesto. Return the shellfish to the saucepan, cover and cook a further minute just to heat through. Serve with boiled rice or crusty french bread. Serves 4.

Smart Saucery

If you want pan-fried fish to be crispy on the outside, cook it over a high heat in a little butter until lightly browned and just cooked inside. If you are looking for more of a steamed effect, cook the fish over high heat for about 30 seconds in a little butter just to seal the base, then cover tightly, reduce the heat and cook until white droplets form on the top surface of the fish and the flesh changes colour.
I prefer to pan-cook most of my fish covered, especially the delicate species, as it seems to keep the fish moist. There's no chance of it falling apart, because you don't have to turn it.

Pan-fried Fish with Avocado Sauce

Restaurants often serve up fish with the sauce cooked in the pan, it's very easy, just ensure the avocados are good quality.

Preparation Time: 5 minutes
Cooking Time: 10 minutes

4 fillets medium-textured fresh fish, eg cod,
 maumau, tarakihi and john dory
flour to dredge
1 tbsp oil
2 tbsp lemon juice
¼ cup plain fromage frais or sour cream
1 avocado, pureed or mashed
½ tsp crushed garlic
2 tbsp finely chopped parsley
salt and freshly ground black pepper to taste
pinch of chilli powder

Dredge the fish in flour and shake to remove excess. Heat the oil in a frypan and cook the fish over a medium heat until opaque, or until it begins to flake in the deepest part. Remove from the pan and keep warm. Add the lemon juice and fromage frais to the pan and stir until smooth. Mix in the avocado, garlic and parsley. Season to taste with salt, pepper and chilli powder. Spoon over the fish and serve immediately. Serves 4.

Pan-fried Salmon Steaks with a Light Fume and Brie Sauce

This is one of the most popular recipes I served while working at the New Zealand pavilion of the 1993 Hong Kong Food Service Show. It's quick and easy and the blend of wine and cheese forms a light coating sauce.

Preparation Time: 5 minutes
Cooking Time: 3–4 minutes

700–800g fresh salmon, skin on, or 4 salmon steaks
salt and freshly ground black pepper
2 tbsp butter
1 cup fume blanc or sauvignon blanc wine
about 130g diced salmon brie or plain brie, rind
 removed
1 spring onion, finely minced
optional garnish: curled spring onion tops

Buy deboned salmon or use tweezers to remove the central bones from the fillet. If using a side of salmon, cut diagonally into steaks about 2cm thick. Season with salt and pepper. Heat the butter in a large pan and place salmon in the pan skin side down. Cook for about 1 minute to lightly crisp the skin. Pour over the wine and slice over the cheese, mixing it into the liquid where possible. Sprinkle over the spring onion. Cover tightly and cook about 2 minutes. The fish is cooked when white droplets appear on the surface. Serve salmon at once with a little sauce poured over. Garnish with finely shredded spring onion tops chilled in iced water until they curl. Serves 4.

Pan-fried Fish with Spicy Cashew Sauce

This lightly spicy cashew sauce makes a great partner for fish fillets, steaks and whole roasted fish.

Prep Time 5 minutes plus at least 1 hour marinating
Cooking Time: 6–8 minutes

6 large medium or firm-textured fish fillets
salt and freshly ground black pepper
2 tbsp butter

Cashew Sauce

1 tbsp oil
1 tsp crushed garlic

Pan Fried Fish with Avocado Sauce and Greek Salad

2 tsp garam masala
1 tbsp hot chilli sauce
400ml tin coconut cream
100g roasted, salted cashew nuts
salt and pepper to taste

Prepare the sauce before cooking the fish. In a saucepan, heat the oil and cook the garlic and garam masala for a few seconds. Add the chilli sauce and coconut cream and bring to a simmer. Crush the cashew nuts in a bag using a bottle or rolling pin, then add to sauce. Cook over very low heat until thick (it catches easily). Season to taste. Pan fry the fish and serve with sauce. Serves 6.

Mango Prawns from Hell

This is one of my favourite seafood recipes. Don't be put off by the long list of ingredients — they all go into a blender together to create a wonderfully exotic sauce. It goes fantastically with virtually any type of seafood — whole roasted fish, pan-fried fillets, grilled or barbecued seafood, you name it, it's all divine!

Preparation Time: 10 minutes
Cooking Time: 5 minutes

Sauce

1 ripe mango, peeled and chopped
1 chilli pepper, seeded and chopped
1–2 tsp tabasco or other hot pepper sauce (to taste)
2 large cloves garlic, peeled and chopped
1 tbsp finely chopped root ginger
¼ cup fine coconut
½ tsp each of ground coriander and cumin
½ cup tinned coconut cream
¼ cup lemon juice
3 tbsp chopped fresh coriander leaves

2 tbsp peanut oil
1 red and 1 yellow pepper, finely diced
50–60 large raw prawns, peeled and deveined

Puree all the sauce ingredients. Transfer the mixture to a saucepan and simmer for 3 minutes. Heat the peanut oil and cook the peppers for 2–3 minutes until their colour changes. Add the mango sauce and bring to a simmer. Mix in the prawns and cook for about 2 minutes, stirring frequently, just until prawns change colour. Do not overcook. Serve on a bed of rice or crispy noodles. Serves 6–8 as a main course allowing 7–8 prawns per person.
NB Recipe can easily be halved or served with other seafood, eg grilled or panfried fish steaks or fillets.

Tahitian Fish Sandwich

Salsa Seafood Partners

When you think salsa, don't just think of spicy Mexican tomato brews.
Salsas come in endless varieties — peach and mint, kiwifruit and pawpaw,
orange and avocado are just some fresh salsa combinations. Salsas are generally
made with raw or lightly cooked fruit or vegetables and have a chunky sauce-like
texture. They make an excellent partner for a quick seafood grill or pan-fry and
are also good with any type of grilled or barbecued chicken or meat.
Convenience products such as pesto and taco sauce, are ideal for adding intense
flavours to simple, fresh salsa ingredients. Create your own salsa tastes by
using these recipes as a guideline. Many salsas can be prepared in advance
and will keep for 1–2 days in the fridge.

Mexican Tomato Salsa

Blend together 4–5 large peeled and chopped tomatoes,
½ cup commercial taco sauce, 2 tbsp chopped fresh
coriander. Season to taste. Chill until required. Salsa
will keep in the fridge for 2–3 days.

Peach and Mint Salsa

Finely dice 3 peaches, mix with 2 tbsp lemon juice,
2 tbsp finely chopped mint, ½ finely chopped spring
onion and a little salt and pepper to taste. Serve within
2 hours or salsa will discolour.

Chunky Guacamole Salsa

Dice 1 large avocado and mix with 2 finely diced
tomatoes, ½ finely chopped red onion, 1 tsp crushed
garlic and the juice of ½ lemon. Season with salt and
freshly ground black pepper to taste. Serve within 2
hours or salsa will discolour.

Kiwifruit and Pawpaw Salsa

Finely dice ½ a pawpaw or melon and 4 kiwifruit.
Combine with ¼ cup finely chopped red onion, 2 tbsp
chopped coriander, the juice of 2 limes and ¼ tsp
tabasco sauce. Season to taste with salt and freshly

ground black pepper. Chill until required. Salsa will keep in the fridge for 1 day.

Fresh Banana Salsa

Combine 2 small mashed bananas, 1 tbsp lemon juice, ¼ cup toasted thread coconut, pinch each of salt and freshly ground black pepper and 1 tbsp minced lemon-grass (optional). Serve within 1 hour or salsa will discolour.

Corn and Pepper Salsa

Mix 1 cup cooked kernel corn with ½ cup finely diced red or green pepper, 2 tbsp chopped mint or coriander, ½ tsp crushed garlic, a pinch of chilli powder, salt and freshly ground black pepper to taste and 1 tbsp oil. Chill until required. Salsa will keep in the fridge for 2–3 days.

Tahitian Fish Sandwich with Fresh Banana Salsa

For a casual lunch or supper I quite often serve hot fish sandwiches. In the time it takes fish to cook you can have everything else prepared.

Preparation Time: 10 minutes
Cooking Time: 4–5 minutes

2 tbsp butter
optional: 2 tbsp chopped green peppercorns

Whole Baked Fish Sandwiches

A whole baked or roasted fish hot with a selection of sandwich fixings and some flavoured homemade mayonnaise is ideal for casual entertaining. Allow your guests to assemble their own combinations.

4 boneless fillets of fresh fish
salt and freshly ground black pepper to season
juice of ½ a lemon
4 pieces of focaccia bread, baps or rolls
⅓ cup mayonnaise
¼ cup finely chopped coriander
8–10 washed lettuce leaves, a handful of snowpea shoots
1 avocado, sliced
banana salsa (see recipe above)

Heat the butter and add the peppercorns and lightly seasoned fish fillets. Cook for about 2 minutes on each side until the fish is just cooked through. Squeeze over the lemon juice. Split the focaccia or baps. Mix the mayonnaise and coriander and spread on both cut sides of each piece of bread. Top with lettuce, snowpea shoots, avocado, hot fish and a dollop of banana salsa. Makes 8 pieces, serve 2 per person.

Stir-frying Seafood

Most of us leave seafood stir-fries to the Chinese, because their dishes always taste fabulous and never fall apart. The reason for this last attribute is that they coat the fish lightly with cornflour before cooking which provides a protective layer that withstands the rigours of stir-frying. The stable texture of squid, mussels and prawns don't require this treatment. Take care not to overcook when stir-frying any seafood as some fish fall apart, while other seafood species become tough and dry.

Chilli Garlic Prawns

Prawns can vary tremendously in quality — some can be quite mushy. There's no real way of knowing before you buy, but mixing the prawns with a little cornflour and running them under cold water for 10–15 minutes is an old Chinese trick that ensures perfect crisp crunchy prawns.

Preparation Time: 5 minutes plus marinating
Cooking Time: 3–4 minutes

30–40 large raw prawns
1 tbsp sweet chilli sauce
2 tsp crushed garlic
2 tbsp lemon juice
¼ cup olive oil or melted butter

Mix the prawns with all the ingredients, except the oil or butter, and refrigerate for at least 15 minutes. Heat the oil and stir-fry the prawns until they turn pink (3–4 minutes). Alternatively, thread 2–3 prawns onto soaked skewers and grill over charcoal or barbecue, brushing with melted butter or oil. Serves 6–8.

Spicy Squid and Asparagus Stir-fry

Stir-fried King Prawns and Squid

Spicy Squid and Asparagus Stir-fry

Preparation Time: 15 minutes
Cooking Time: 5 minutes

2–3 large squid tubes
2 tbsp oil
1 tsp crushed garlic
1 tsp freshly ground black pepper
1 tbsp chilli sauce
1–2 tbsp soy sauce
500g blanched asparagus (or green beans or broccoli)
3 spring onions, finely sliced
1 red pepper, finely diced

Remove the membrane from the squid tubes and slice into 1cm strips. Heat the oil in a wok or frypan. Cook the garlic for 30 seconds, then add the freshly ground black pepper and squid. Stir-fry the squid for 1 minute or until it turns white. Remove the squid and set aside. Add the chilli, soy sauce, asparagus, spring onions and red pepper. Stir-fry for 2 minutes. Return the squid to the wok, cook a further minute until tender, then serve immediately. Serves 4. Serve with rice or crispy noodles.

Crispy noodles are available from supermarkets and Asian food stores. To make your own, simply deep fry dry noodles until they puff and crisp. Drain on brown paper and use the same day.

Stir-fried King Prawns and Squid

This succulent stir-fry needs to be cooked at the last minute. As long as everything is ready it only takes 5–6 minutes to cook. The most important thing is not to overcook it.

Preparation Time: 10 minutes
Cooking Time: 5–6 minutes

500g squid tubes
2 tbsp sesame oil
12–16 large, unshelled prawns
3 tbsp oyster sauce
juice of 1 lemon
2 tsp crushed garlic
salt and freshly ground black pepper to season
garnish: chopped fresh coriander

Cut the squid into small triangles and lightly score in diamond patterns with a sharp knife . Heat the oil in a large frypan, wok or barbecue. When very hot, toss the squid for 2–3 minutes until it turns white. Remove from the pan. Add the prawns, oyster sauce, lemon juice, garlic and salt and pepper and toss for 2 minutes to cook through. Return the squid to the pan to heat through for 1 minute. Serve immediately, garnished with fresh coriander. Serves 4.

Variations:
Extend the stir-fry with lightly cooked vegetables, eg peppers, mushrooms, beans, snowpeas and spring onions.

Fresh Fish and Vegetable Toss

This delicious stir-fry works equally well with prawns, mussels or squid. The combination of seasonings and fresh coriander provide a wonderful flavour.

Preparation Time: 5 minutes
Cooking Time: 5 minutes

3 fillets boneless tarakihi or ling (about 600g)
1 tsp cornflour
2 tbsp olive oil (eg Sapio or Bertolli, not virgin)
1 bunch green beans or asparagus, cut in thin diagonal slices
1 red pepper, cut into thin strips
¼ cup soy sauce
1 tbsp rice or white wine vinegar or balsamic vinegar
1 tsp sugar
1 spring onion, finely chopped
3 tbsp chopped fresh coriander
salt and pepper to taste

Cut the fish into 1.5cm thick strips on a slight angle, about 1.5 cm thick. Shake in the cornflour. Heat the oil in a wok or heavy pan and fry the beans and peppers for about 1 minute to soften. Add the fish and toss for about 1 minute, then add all the other ingredients, stir to coat, cover and cook about 2–3 minutes until fish is just cooked- it should just flake. Do not stir too much at this point or the fish may break up. Serve at once on a bed of rice or noodles. Serves 3–4.

Mediterranean Stir-fried Squid

Squid responds well to a wide variety of marinades. This simple one delivers the light, clean tastes of the Mediterranean.

Preparation Time: 10 minutes plus marinating
Cooking Time: 2–3 minutes

4 squid tubes (approx 400g)
¼ cup olive oil
2 tbsp lemon juice
1 tsp crushed garlic
2 tbsp chopped fresh rosemary
salt and freshly ground black pepper
2 tbsp herb pesto

Open the squid tubes by slicing down one side, then remove any cartilage and rinse well. Use a sharp knife to lightly score squid on the outside in a diamond pattern. Cut into strips about 1.5cm wide. Combine all other ingredients, except pesto, and marinate squid for at least 30 minutes, turning occasionally (squid can be marinated up to 24 hours in this mixture). Drain squid and cook in an oiled pan or wok over high heat, tossing for about 2 minutes until flesh has whitened. Mix in the pesto. The squid is cooked when the flesh turns from opaque to white and becomes tender — overcooking it will make it tough. Serves 4.

Mediterranean Squid (Pg 58)

Menu

Busy Mid Week Dinner

Spicy Squid and Asparagus Stir Fry

Perfect Rice

Tangelos in Caramel Syrup

Preparation
1 Put rice on to cook.
2 Prepare squid and asparagus stir fry ingredients.
3 Prepare dessert.

Suggested Wine
Chilled Riesling

French Mussel and Fennel Pan

Menu

Goats Cheese, Olives and Croutons

French Mussel and Fennel Pan

Focaccia bread

Tamarillo Clafoutis

Preparation
1 Make or buy focaccia bread
2 Prepare French Mussel and Fennel Pan; ready to cook
3 Prepare and cook the dessert

Suggested Wine
Sauvignon Blanc

French Mussel and Fennel Pan

Salvador Dali once made the comment 'food that only a battle to peel makes it vulnerable to the conquest of our palate'. There's certainly something satisfying about extracting tender mussels from their shells, especially these ones redolent with the flavours of south west France.

Preparation Time: 15 minutes
Cooking Time: 10–12 minutes

2 tbsp butter
1 onion, finely sliced
1 florence fennel bulb*, finely sliced
1 tbsp tomato paste
½ tsp crushed garlic
2 tbsp pernod
½ cup wine
optional: good pinch saffron
400g tin tomatoes in juice, pureed
about 3 dozen mussels, scrubbed and beards removed
1 cup water
salt and pepper

Heat the butter in a large saucepan. Add the onion and fennel and cook until soft. Add the tomato paste and garlic and cook for a further 30 seconds. Add the pernod, wine, optional saffron, tomatoes and mussels. Cover the pot tightly and cook until the mussels open, removing them to a deep-sided serving dish as they do. Once all are cooked, add the water to the pan juices, heat. Season to taste. Pour over the mussels. Serves 4.

* Fennel bulbs can be purchased from good super-markets or greengrocers

Veracruz Fish Bake

Great for a casual dinner with friends this easy fish bake is light and spicy with Mexican flavours.

Preparation Time: 10 minutes
Cooking Time: 20 minutes

600g or 8 fresh boneless fish fillets eg hapuku, monkfish or bluenose
¼ cup olive oil
1 large onion, finely chopped
3 cloves garlic, crushed
1 tsp chilli paste
400g tin tomatoes in juice, chopped
3 bottled jalapeno peppers, drained, seeded and cut in thin strips
juice of 1 orange and ½ tsp finely grated orange rind
juice of 1 lemon
about 2 tbsp butter
garnish: ¼ cup chopped fresh coriander

Arrange the fillets in a single layer in a lightly greased baking dish. Lightly score each fillet with a sharp knife. In a pan heat the oil and cook the onion, garlic and chilli paste until tender but not browned. Add the tomatoes, peppers, juices and the rind and bring to a simmer. Pour over the fish. Dot with butter, cover and bake at 200°C for about 20 minutes or until fish is cooked through. Garnish with coriander. Serves 4.

Fish Parcels

Wrapping it up

Coatings, whether pastry, tinfoil, parchment or leaves such as spinach,
serve to enclose flavours and retain moisture. Individual servings of fish
wrapped in baking paper or tinfoil provide a tantalising experience of
mouthwatering aromas as the packages are opened. Seafood packages can be
prepared ahead of time and chilled until ready to cook.
Individual packages will take about 10–12 minutes to cook in a 250°C oven. They
are cooked when they start to puff. Tinfoil seafood parcels cook well on the
barbecue. Sit them on a pre-heated hot plate and cook for 5–6 minutes until they puff.

Mexican Fish Parcels

Preparation Time: 10 minutes
Cooking Time: 8–12 minutes

*4 boneless medium-textured fish fillets, eg cod,
  snapper, dory, tarakihi*
4 pieces tinfoil, 20cm×30cm
½ cup taco sauce
100g shrimps
salt and freshly ground black pepper
optional: 2 tbsp chopped coriander
1 lemon, cut in quarters

Place each fillet on a piece of foil. Spread each piece
with taco sauce, and divide the shrimps over the top.
Sprinkle with salt, black pepper and optional coriander.
Pull up the sides of the foil and fold over the top and
sides to enclose and seal. Place joined-edge facing
upwards on a baking tray, and bake at 220°C for 8–12
minutes, or until the packages puff. To serve, slit the
package across the top and open. Accompany with
lemon wedges. Serves 4. Serving Suggestion: accompany with baked potatoes and a crisp green salad.

69

Oriental Fish Parcels

Preparation Time: 10 minutes
Cooking Time: 6–8 minutes

100g thinly sliced vegetables, eg carrots, leeks,
  peppers
4 boneless fish fillets
4 squares tin foil (20cm×20cm)
2 tsp sesame oil
1 tsp crushed root ginger
½ tsp cornflour
1 spring onion, finely sliced

Blanch the vegetables in boiling water for 1 minute,
then drain and cool under cold water. Place a fillet on
each piece of foil and top with the vegetables. Mix the
oil, ginger, cornflour and spring onions. Divide among
the parcels. Pull up the sides to form a parcel, pinch
the top and seal to make a purse shape. Place parcels
on an oven tray and bake for 10–12 minutes in a pre-
heated 220°C oven. Serves 4.

To Prepare Fish in Parcels

Foil parcels: Cut squares of tin foil about 20cm
by 20cm. Place the filling in the centre, pull up
the sides and fold at the top to form a sealed purse
shape.

Paper parcels: Use baking paper or greaseproof.
Cut into circles of about 22–24cms. Fold each
circle in half and cut paper at the top to form the
circle into a heart shape. Place the filling slightly
to one side of the centre. Fold over the paper to
meet the other side evenly. Working around the
edge make small folds until the parcel is sealed.

Other Fish Parcel Combinations

• tomatoes, peppers and pesto
• cooked leeks, garlic, tomatoes and fennel seeds
• wilted spinach, orange and tarragon
• banana, coconut, coriander and lemon juice

One Dish Fish Dinners

A single dish served at the table is an easy and informal way
to entertain. Hearty, filling fare, such as paella and smoked fish and kumara pie
need nothing more than a crisp green salad as accompaniment.

Smoked Fish and Kumara Pie

For a rainy Sunday lunch or dinner when the weather
is foul, a flavoursome fish pie delivers the necessary
level of comfort. Mashed kumara makes a great addition to the topping, its sweetness balancing perfectly
with the smoked fish and cheesy sauce.

Preparation Time: 20 minutes
Cooking Time: 15–20 minutes

2 medium kumara and 2 potatoes, peeled and cut
  into small chunks
5 tbsp butter
1 large onion, finely sliced
1 stalk celery, finely diced
¼ cup flour
3 cups milk
½ tsp each of ground black pepper and nutmeg
450g flaked, fresh smoked fish or 450g tin smoked

fish, drained and flaked
2 cups cooked rice (optional but a good extender)
1 cup grated tasty cheddar cheese

Cook the kumara and potato in boiling salted water for
about 15 minutes until tender. Melt the butter in a
heavy based saucepan. Cook the onion and celery for
5 minutes until soft. Stir in the flour and cook for 1
minute. Remove from the heat. Gradually add the milk
stirring continuously. Return to the heat, stirring constantly until the sauce thickens and comes to the boil.
Stir in the pepper, nutmeg, flaked smoked fish and rice.
Place the mixture in a greased medium oven-proof dish.
Drain kumara and potato and mash with a little milk,
seasoning to taste with salt and pepper. Spread over
the fish mixture. Sprinkle the cheese over the topping.
(Dish can be prepared ahead to this point). Bake at
200°C for 15–20 minutes until golden brown or cover
and microwave for 5 minutes, then place under a grill
to brown. Serves 4–5.

Paella

Paella

This recipe is adapted from one given to me by Serafin Bueno, now resident in Spain who is stacking up Michelin stars. It's a great dish for a crowd, delivering heaps of flavour and satisfaction.

Preparation Time: 10 minutes
Cooking Time: 30 minutes

3 tbsp olive oil
1 onion, finely diced
1 tbsp crushed garlic
2 tsp each of turmeric and paprika
2 bayleaves, crumbled
2 cups shortgrain rice
700g seafood eg diced fish, mussels in shell, prawns, squid, etc
130g tin capsicum, or 1 red pepper, finely diced
400g tin tomatoes in juice, diced
4 cups each of fish or chicken stock, and boiling water
garnish: lemon wedges, chopped parsley, 2 tbsp sherry

Heat the oil in a large, shallow ovenproof pan or a frypan with a heatproof handle. Add the onion and cook for about 5 minutes until soft. Add the garlic, turmeric, paprika and bay leaves. Cook for 1 minute. Add the rice and fry for 2–3 minutes, stirring over the heat. Mix in the capsicum, tomatoes and juice (dish can be prepared ahead to this point). Stir in the boiling water,

chicken stock, then place the seafood on top of the rice, pressing it in a little. Bake covered at 170°C for 20 minutes. Remove from the oven, and stand for 10 minutes. Decorate with lemon wedges and parsley, and pour over sherry just before serving. Serves 5–6.

Optional additions: diced chicken, sliced Julia Colbasse sausages and peas make this into a traditional party paella.

Menu

Sunday Lunch with Friends and Neighbours

Platter of Crusty Bread with Tapenade, Pesto, Goat's Cheese, Cherry Tomatoes and Crusty Bread

Paella

Mixed Green Salad with Roasted Walnuts

Tiramisu

Preparation
1 Prepare ingredients for salad, wash and dry salad greens, roast walnuts, roast peppers, prepare dressing
2 Prepare paella ingredients
3 Prepare dessert

Suggested Wine
Chilled Riesling or Chardonnay

Cooking Whole Fish

Fish, like meat and poultry tastes better cooked on the bone, staying moister and to my mind retaining more flavour. If you have any misgivings about cooking a whole fish, for fear you won't know when its cooked or how to deal with it once it is, forget them. Timing a whole fish is very simple — when the eye turns white and the flesh no longer feels bouncy when you press it in the deepest part behind the fins, the fish is cooked. When it comes to serving just bring to mind the anatomy of a fish — many species have a row of very fine bones around the top and bottom edges and a short line of bones up the centre of each fillet. Use a flat thin bladed spatula and the flesh will slide from the bones very easily. Allow a 1–1.2 kg whole fish for every 2 people.

Whole Maumau Baked in Ginger and Coconut

If you ever see fresh maumau, buy them. They are one of my favourite fish with a delicious sweet flesh and medium flake. Cook them whole as in this recipe or use the fillets as you might any medium-textured fish — pan-fried, steamed or baked.

Preparation Time: 5 minutes plus marinating
Cooking Time: 6–8 minutes

4 small maumau or snapper (about 400–500g each)
400ml can coconut cream
2 tbsp minced fresh root ginger
2 tsp garam masala
1 tsp salt
½ tsp white pepper

Scale and clean the fish and slash in a diagonal pattern with a sharp knife to from a criss cross pattern on both sides. In a big roasting dish mix the coconut cream, garam masala and salt and pepper. Turn the fish in the coconut mixture , rubbing the mixture into the cuts. Leave to marinate for about 30 minutes. Preheat the oven to 250°C and bake the fish for 6–8 minutes, depending on size, until the eyes turn white and the flesh meets no resistance when pressed in the deepest part. Lift out the fish and thicken the sauce if desired with a teaspoon of cornflour thinned to a paste with a little water. Serve 1 fish per person and spoon the sauce into a jug for each person to pour over. N B: this method can also be used successfully for larger fish — allow approximately 5 minutes per 1cm of thickness.

Hot Roasted Whole Spiced Fish

This sensational fish recipe was conceived on a recent yachting holiday up in Fiji's Yasawa islands. As long as the fish is really fresh any species will do.

Preparation Time: 15 minutes
Cooking Time: 30–35 minutes

2–2.5kg whole fish, cleaned and scaled

Flavour paste

1 tbsp chilli sauce
1 tsp garam masala
2 tbsp oil
1 clove garlic, crushed

Make slashes on either side of the fish in diamond patterns. Combine the flavour paste ingredients and rub over both sides of the fish and in the cavity. Place in an oiled roasting dish and bake at 220°C for 30–55 minutes until fish eye turns white and there is no resistance when flesh is pressed on the thickest part. Do not over-cook. Serves 6.

Accompany with Rice, and Paw Paw, Avocado and Pepper Salad (see page 35).

Chargrilled Whole Fish Wrapped in Leaves

Preparation Time: 15 minutes
Cooking Time: 20–35 minutes

1 medium-sized whole fresh fish, e.g. snapper, about 1.5kg, cleaned, gutted and scaled
1 large bunch fresh herbs, e.g. parsley, thyme, basil, oregano, coriander or dill
1 tbsp butter
1 lemon, sliced thinly
freshly ground black pepper
10–12 fresh spinach leaves or sorrel leaves or a couple of banana leaves to wrap fish

Slash the fish deeply on the diagonal 3 or 4 times on each side. Place all the ingredients except the spinach leaves in the cavity of the fish. Lightly oil and preheat

Chargrilled Whole Fish Wrapped in Leaves

the grill or preheat the oven to 250°C. Wrap the fish in spinach leaves, large herb leaves, banana leaves or soaked lotus leaves and cook over medium heat, about 10cm above the heat source, for 10 minutes on each side. If you have a covered grill, larger fish can be cooked successfully; without a cover larger fish tend to cook unevenly.

If cooking in the oven bake the fish at 250°C for about 30 minutes. The fish is cooked when the eye has turned white and the flesh gives when pressed at its deepest point.

Grilled Fish with Thai Seasonings

In place of lemon, herbs and butter, mix together 2 tsp crushed garlic, 2 tbsp chilli sauce, 2 tbsp oil or clarified butter and 2 tbsp chopped fresh basil or coriander. Brush the inside of the fish cavity and the slashed sides before cooking with this mixture.

Menu

A Weekend Barbecue at the Beach

Chargrilled Whole Fish Wrapped in Leaves
Focaccia or Texan Corn Bread
Ember-baked Potatoes
Greek Salad

Preparation
1 Prepare fish ready for cooking
2 Make Bread
3 Wrap potatoes individually in tinfoil and make Greek Salad

Suggested Wine
Chilled Fume Blanc

Poultry

'Poultry is to the cook what canvas is to the painter.'
Brillat Savarin's testimony sums up the sheer versatility of our favourite bird. The world over, few foods can match chicken for variety and ease of cooking.
Today's poultry comes in a range of prepared cuts that make life even easier for the busy cook. Some people can cook delicious chicken while others always deliver a dryish, tough result. The breast meat of all birds is vulnerable to overcooking as it is so lean. Unless you are dealing with a broiler, cook poultry quickly using a high heat. Marinades also add tenderness and flavour.

Chicken Skewers Marinated with Yoghurt and Indian Spices; Spicy Chicken Mole; Chicken with Lemon and Herbs

Make It Spicy

Chicken Skewers Marinated with Yoghurt and Indian Spices

The yoghurt used in this spicy marinade makes the chicken melt in your mouth. This marinade is also suitable for grilled chicken thighs and whole breasts, whole birds and barbecues.

Preparation Time: 10 minutes plus marinating
Cooking Time: 8–10 minutes

4 single chicken breasts, cut in 3cm dice

Marinade

2 tbsp unsweetened natural yoghurt
grated rind and juice of 1 lemon or lime
1 tbsp chilli sauce — Thai brand
1 tsp each of paprika, cumin, garam masala,
* crushed garlic*
½ tsp each of ground ginger
8–10 wooden skewers soaked in water
salt and pepper to taste

Combine the chicken with the yoghurt and spices. Allow to marinate for at least 2 hours in the fridge (or up to 8 hours). Preheat the oven to 220°C. Thread the chicken onto soaked skewers. Place on a baking tray and season with salt and pepper. Bake or grill for about 10 minutes until the chicken feels very springy when pressed and the juices run clear. Stand for 5 minutes before serving. Accompany with rice, poppadoms, fresh banana salad (see page 113). Serves 4.

Spicy Chicken Mole
(in an aromatic sauce with peppers and spices)

Simple to prepare, yet spicy and exotic in taste, this chicken dish makes great dinner party or buffet fare. It can be prepared a day ahead and baked when needed.

Preparation Time: 10 minutes
Cooking Time: 25–30 minutes

1 tbsp oil
1 small onion, finely diced
1 tsp each of ground cumin and sugar
1 tsp chilli paste or powder
2 tsp crushed garlic
1 tsp fennel seeds
400g tin tomatoes in juice

400ml chicken stock or 1 can chicken broth made
* up to 400ml with water*
130g tin capsicum, drained, or ½ red pepper, diced
4 squares dark semi-sweet chocolate
salt and black pepper
2 tbsp oil
6 chicken legs
garnish: finely diced red pepper and fresh coriander

In a medium saucepan, heat the oil over a medium heat and cook the onion, spices and flavourings until the onion is soft (about 5 minutes). Add the tomatoes, chicken stock and capsicum and simmer for 10 minutes. Mix in the chocolate and stir until smooth. Remove the sauce from the heat and season to taste with salt and pepper. Puree the sauce until smooth (recipe can be prepared ahead to this point). In a separate pan heat the oil and brown chicken well all over. Place the chicken in a baking dish, pour over the sauce, cover and bake at 200°C for 25–30 minutes. Garnish with red pepper and coriander. Serves 6.

Chicken and Bean Pan-fry

This easy chicken pan-fry makes a great filler for tortillas, tacos or pita bread.

Preparation Time: 10 minutes
Cooking Time: 15 minutes

2 tbsp oil
400g boneless chicken, cut into thin strips
1 medium onion, finely diced
2 tbsp tomato paste
1 tsp crushed garlic
1 tbsp ground cumin
¼ cup sweet chilli sauce
½ cup water
1 cup prepared pasta sauce
310g tin red kidney beans, rinsed and drained
salt and pepper to taste
150g reduced-fat sour cream
garnish: 2–3 tbsp chopped coriander

Heat the oil and brown the chicken in batches. Reserve. Add the onion and tomato paste and cook over a medium heat until the onion is soft. Add the garlic and cumin and cook a further minute. Mix in the chilli sauce, water, pasta sauce and kidney beans. Season to taste with salt and pepper. Return the chicken to the pan and simmer for 5 minutes. Remove from the heat and mix in the sour cream. Garnish with coriander. Serves 4.

Chicken and Noodles with Chilli Peanut Sauce

A delicate creamy, peanuty curry that even those who don't like chillies will enjoy.

Preparation Time: 10 minutes
Cooking Time: 12–15 minutes

400g egg noodles
1 tbsp vegetable oil or sesame oil
2 tsp crushed garlic
500g chicken schnitzel or boneless chicken thighs,
  cut into strips
1 cup coconut cream (freeze the rest for later use)
2 tbsp each of sweet chilli sauce and peanut butter
3 tbsp soy sauce
1 pepper, red or green, chopped

Cook the noodles according to manufacturer's instructions. Heat the oil in a large wok or frypan. Add the garlic and cook for 30 seconds. Add the chicken and stir-fry over high heat for 2–3 minutes until lightly browned. Combine the coconut cream, chilli sauce, peanut butter and soy sauce. Mix into the chicken and simmer for a further 2–3 minutes. Mix in the cooked, drained noodles. Stir-fry for 2–3 minutes to heat through and coat. Serves 4.

Chicken and Spinach Curry

Great for a quick healthy meal-in-one, this curry uses frozen spinach for ease of preparation.

Preparation Time: 5 minutes
Cooking Time: 8–10 minutes

1 large onion, finely diced
1 tbsp oil
2 tsp crushed garlic
1–2 tbsp green curry paste (to taste)
1 cinnamon quill
pinch of ground cloves
½ pkt frozen spinach, thawed (or a large bunch
  spinach, blanched and squeezed dry)
1 cup chicken stock
400g–500g boneless chicken thighs, sliced into thin
  strips
½ cup cream
salt and pepper

Cook the onion in the oil in a large pan over a medium heat until tender. Add the garlic and curry paste and sizzle a few more seconds. Mix in the cinnamon quill, cloves, spinach and stock and bring to a simmer. Add the chicken and cream and simmer for 6–8 minutes until the chicken is cooked through. Season to taste, lift out the cinnamon quill and discard. Serves 4–5.

Chicken and Noodles with Chilli Peanut Sauce

Menu

Crostini Platter

Spicy Chicken Mole

Cornbread

Mixed Salad Greens with Peppers and Avocado

Fresh Peaches with Ginger Crumble

Preparation
1 Make cornbread.
2 Make crostini bases, prepare toppings.
3 Prepare spicy chicken mole ingredients, make the sauce.
4 Wash and prepare salad ingredients (add avocado just before serving.)
5 Assemble crostini platter.
6 Finish cooking spicy chicken mole.
7 Assemble and cook dessert.

Suggested Wine
Dry Gerwurztraminer

Thai Chicken Curry

Chicken Schnitzels

Buy store-prepared chicken schnitzels, or make your own by flattening chicken breasts or thighs between 2 sheets of plastic wrap. They can be pan-fried, grilled or barbecued.

Chicken with Lemon and Herbs

Flattened boneless chicken breasts or thighs take just a few minutes to cook over high heat. A range of marinades can be used, this one is light and aromatic with flavours of lemon, thyme and ginger.

Preparation Time: 10 minutes plus marinating
Cooking Time: 5–7 minutes

5 boneless chicken thighs or 4 single boneless chicken breasts
finely grated rind and juice of 1 lemon
3 tbsp oil
2 tbsp fresh ginger, finely chopped, or 1½ tsp ground ginger
2 tbsp chopped fresh thyme or 1 tsp dry thyme
salt and pepper

Place each breast or thigh between plastic wrap and flatten to a thin schnitzel using a rolling pin or other heavy, flat implement. Combine all the remaining ingredients and mix through the chicken. Marinate for at least 15 minutes or up to 4 hours in the fridge. Barbecue, pan fry or grill for 5–7 minutes until chicken is golden and cooked. Accompany with Watercress and Mushroom Salad (see page 113 for recipe). Serves 4.

Sesame Schnitzels with Fresh Banana Salsa

Sesame seeds make a delicious crunchy coating that is a great change from flour or breadcrumbs.

Preparation Time: 10 minutes plus 10 minutes chilling
Cooking Time: 4 minutes

4 chicken schnitzels
¼ cup flour seasoned with a little salt and pepper
1 egg, lightly beaten
½ cup sesame seeds
about 2 tbsp oil to cook
1 recipe banana salsa (see page 65)
garnish: fresh coriander

Shake the schnitzels in the flour, dip in the egg, then in the sesame seeds to coat. Chill in fridge for 10 minutes to set seeds. Heat the oil and fry the meat on both sides until lightly golden. Serve with banana salsa (recipe page 65) and garnish with coriander. Serves 4.

Thai Chicken Curry

This makes a great dinner party or buffet dish, as the sauce can be prepared in advance. Green curry paste keeps well in the freezer, just cut as required.

Preparation Time: 10 minutes
Cooking Time: 15–18 minutes

1kg boneless chicken thighs, thinly sliced
2 tbsp green curry paste
2 tbsp oil
1 large onion, finely diced
1 tsp each of crushed garlic and paprika
400ml tin coconut cream
2 cups chicken stock
2 tbsp minced lemongrass or finely grated rind of ½ lemon
optional: 6–8 dried curry leaves
salt and pepper to taste
garnish: sliced spring onions, sliced peppers, ½ cup toasted cashew nuts

Mix together the chicken and green curry paste. Reserve in the fridge while cooking the sauce. In a large heavy saucepan heat the oil and cook the onion until tender. Add the garlic and paprika and sizzle a few seconds more. Mix in the coconut cream, stock, lemongrass and optional curry leaves and simmer for 10 minutes (sauce can be prepared ahead to this point). Add the prepared chicken. Reduce heat to low, cover tightly and leave to cook at lowest possible heat for 5–6 minutes without uncovering until the chicken is cooked. Do not overcook. Season to taste and garnish with spring onion, pepper, and cashew nuts. Serves 8–10 as a main course.

Chicken Stir-Fries

Winter or summer stir-fried chicken dishes are always popular.
Asian sauces such as black bean, hoisin, soy, oyster or chilli sauce,
make simple, delicious flavourings for a range of Asian-styled stir-fries.
Alternatively, create stir-fries in other ethnic styles — go Mexican with
cumin, chilli and fresh coriander, or Indian with cumin, garam
masala, curry powder and ginger. The key to stir-frying is to
have everything prepared before you start. The basic technique,
regardless of flavourings, remains the same.

Chicken and Broccoli with Black Bean Sauce

Chicken and Broccoli with Black Bean Sauce

Preparation Time: 10 minutes
Cooking Time: 10 minutes

400g chicken thighs, thinly sliced
2 tbsp black bean sauce
1 head broccoli, stems peeled and cut into florets
2 tbsp oil
1 large onion, sliced in thin wedges
1 tsp crushed garlic
1 tsp cornflour mixed with 2 tbsp water
½ packet bean sprouts

Mix the chicken with the black bean sauce. Place the broccoli in a microwave bowl, cover and cook on 100% power for 3 minutes (or steam). Uncover and cool under cold water. Heat the oil in a wok or heavy pan and fry the onion until starting to brown. Add the garlic and chicken and stir-fry until chicken starts to brown. Add the broccoli and thicken with cornflour and water mix. Add the sprouts and stir-fry for 30 seconds before serving. Serves 4.

Menu

Dinner on the Run
(prepared in less than 30 minutes)

Chicken and Broccoli with Black Bean Sauce
Steamed Rice
Gingered Turnips or Yams
Mint and Ginger Melon Salad

Preparation
1 Put the rice on to cook.
2 Prepare the dessert.
3 Prepare all the stir-fry ingredients ready to cook.
4 When rice is 10 minutes away from being ready, cook the turnips and then stir-fry.
5 Prepare the turnips or yams in the microwave or steamer with 2 tbsp grated ginger and 1 tsp sesame oil until just crisp tender. Toss with a little freshly ground black pepper and serve.

Chicken, Baby Corn and Pepper Stir-fry

A low-calorie, fresh-tasting stir-fry with lots of vegetables.

Preparation Time: 10 minutes
Cooking Time: 5–6 minutes

300g chicken thighs, cut into strips
1 ham steak, diced in 1cm chunks
2 tbsp soy sauce
½ tsp each of salt, sugar and sesame oil
300g blanched fresh asparagus or broccoli, cut into florets
2 tbsp oil
400g tin of baby corn, drained
1 red pepper, cut into strips
optional: 1 pkt snowpeas
2 tsp cornflour mixed with 1 tbsp sherry
1 pkt crispy noodles, to serve

Combine the chicken and ham with the soy sauce and seasonings. Blanch the broccoli or asparagus. Heat the oil in a wok or frypan. Stir-fry the chicken mixture over high heat for 2–3 minutes. Add the corn, asparagus or broccoli, pepper and optional snowpeas. Thicken with the cornflour and sherry. Serve on a bed of crispy noodles or rice. Serves 4.

Hint: always preheat a wok over high heat until the oil is shimmering. This sears the meat or chicken, sealing in the juices and allowing the food to cook quickly.

Kashmir Chicken Stir-fry

The heady flavours of India invigorate this light, tender chicken stir-fry.

Preparation Time: 10 minutes plus marinating
Cooking Time: 20 minutes

½ cup plain yoghurt
2 tsp ground cumin
½ tsp each of cardamom, ground cloves and cinnamon
2 tsp crushed garlic
2 tbsp sweet chilli sauce
1 tbsp paprika
juice of 1 lemon
400g–500g boneless chicken thighs, cut in slivers across the grain
2 tbsp oil
garnish: ¼ cup toasted coconut thread

Combine the yoghurt, spices, lemon juice and chicken. Marinate in the fridge for at least 30 minutes (or up to 4 hours). Heat the oil in a heavy pan. Add the chicken and marinade and toss over high heat for 4–5 minutes until it is no longer pink. Mix through coconut threads and serve. Serve with steamed rice and vegetables. Serves 4.

Cantonese Chicken and Vegetables

Oyster sauce provides the mild, smooth flavour that prevails in Cantonese cooking. It makes a great partner with ginger, as in the following easy stir-fry.

Preparation Time: 15 minutes
Cooking Time: 10 minutes

1 tbsp oil
1 large onion, cut into thin segments
1 tbsp finely chopped fresh ginger
1 tsp crushed garlic
½ cup oyster sauce
½ cup water
optional: 1 tbsp hot chilli sauce
500g boneless chicken, thinly sliced
500g dense vegetables, eg strips of red pepper, and carrots
300g light vegetables, eg bean sprouts, snowpeas, sliced cabbage
pepper to taste

Heat the oil in a heavy based pan and cook the onion until soft. Add the ginger and garlic and cook for another minute. Mix in the oyster sauce and water and simmer for 5 minutes. Season to taste with chilli sauce. Add the chicken to the pan and stir in. While the

Cantonese Chicken Stir-fry

chicken simmers, microwave the dense vegetables with 1 tbsp water for 3 minutes or cook in a small amount of water until tender. Add to the chicken with the light vegetables and stir over heat for a further 1–2 minutes until the light vegetables are just wilted. Serve immediately. Serves 4.

Sauteed Chicken Breasts with White Wine, Mushrooms and Tarragon

A subtle mixture of golden chicken breasts infused with the rich flavour of mushrooms in a light, fresh sauce.

Preparation Time: 10 minutes
Cooking Time: 20 minutes

4 boneless, skinless chicken breasts
salt and pepper
2 tbsp butter
2 rashers bacon, diced
300g field mushrooms, sliced
1 tbsp flour
½ cup white wine
1½ cups chicken stock (or use ½ can chicken broth
 mixed with water to make 1½ cups)
1 tsp dried tarragon

Season the chicken breasts with salt and pepper. Melt the butter in a pan and brown chicken on both sides. Remove and reserve. Add the bacon and cook until it starts to brown. Add the mushrooms and cook until dry. Mix in the flour and cook, stirring over heat for about 1 minute. Mix in the wine, stock and tarragon and simmer for 10 minutes. Return the chicken to the pan. Cook for 10 minutes, turning after 5 minutes. Serve on a bed of rice or with creamy whipped potatoes and lightly cooked vegetables. Serves 4.

Saute

Sautes are a quick meal fix for chicken — the meat is lightly browned in the pan, then it is simmered in the sauce ingredients until cooked. The list of flavouring combinations is endless. Try these quick combinations:

• chicken, cashew nuts, red capsicum and snowpeas
• chicken, shrimp and bok choy
• chicken, asparagus and mushrooms

81

Spicy Portuguese Chicken Saute

This spicy chicken saute is a wonderful blend of sweet and hot flavours.

Preparation Time: 10 minutes plus marinating
Cooking Time: 15 minutes

4 single boneless, skinless chicken breasts
salt and freshly ground pepper to season
1 tbsp crushed garlic
1 tbsp oil
2 red and/or yellow peppers, thinly sliced
1 cup prepared pasta sauce
½ cup water
2 tbsp Marsala
1 tsp tabasco or other hot pepper sauce

Season the chicken with salt and pepper and mix with the garlic. Leave to marinate for at least 10 minutes. Heat the oil and fry the chicken until lightly browned all over. Remove and reserve. Add the peppers to the pan and cook until starting to brown. Add the pasta sauce, water, Marsala and chicken, pressing it into the sauce. Simmer for 15 minutes, turning the chicken after 10 minutes. Serve with rice. Serves 4.

Caribbean Chicken

Don't be put off by the long list of ingredients in this recipe, it really stands as a meal-in-one. The wonderful vegetable mixture in this recipe is a great dish on its own. For a great vegetarian entree, try it in a filo pastry parcel.

Preparation Time: 15 minutes
Cooking Time: 30 minutes

4 single skinless, boneless chicken breasts
2 tbsp lemon or lime juice
1 tbsp butter
1 onion, finely sliced
2 kumara, peeled and diced in 1cm pieces
200g pumpkin, peeled and diced in 1cm pieces
¼ cup orange juice
2 tsp each of toasted cumin and fennel seeds
¼ cup toasted thread coconut
salt and pepper
2 tbsp butter
garnish: 2 bananas, diagonally sliced

Flatten the chicken between plastic wrap using a rolling pin or mallet. Mix with the lemon or lime juice and leave to stand while preparing the vegetables. Heat the first quantity of butter in a frypan. Add the onion and cook until just beginning to brown. Add the kumara,

pumpkin and orange juice, cover and cook for 30 minutes or until just tender (you may need to add more liquid if the mixture dries out). Mix in the seeds and coconut, roughly mashing the vegetables. Season well. Meanwhile, heat the second amount of butter, season the chicken and pan-fry for 4–5 minutes on either side or until the juices run clear. Serve the chicken breasts whole or sliced on a bed of vegetables. Garnish with sliced banana. Serves 4.

Kentucky Baked Chicken with Creamy Corn and Thyme Sauce

The light cornmeal coating used here provides a crisp, golden crust that keeps the chicken moist. The recipe sounds rich, but it's not. The chicken is baked and not fried and the sauce is made with milk not cream!

Preparation Time: 15 minutes
Cooking Time: 20 minutes

4 chicken quarters
salt and pepper
1 egg, lightly beaten
about ½ cup cornmeal mixed with a pinch of cayenne to coat
2 tbsp oil

Sauce

3 cobs of corn or 2 cups corn kernels
3 tbsp butter
2 rashers bacon, diced
1 tbsp fresh thyme leaves or ½ tsp dried thyme
2 tbsp flour
1 ½ cups milk
salt, pepper and a pinch of cayenne pepper

Season the chicken with salt and pepper and dip into the egg, then flavoured cornmeal. Put the oil on a flat plate and quickly roll coated pieces in it to coat lightly. Place the chicken in a baking dish and cook at 200°C for about 20 minutes until the coating is crisp and the juices run clear. While the chicken cooks, prepare the sauce. Use a heavy knife to cut the kernels from the fresh corn cobs. Heat the butter and fry the bacon and corn until the bacon starts to brown. Mix in the thyme and flour and cook for 1 minute more. Stir in the milk slowly until the sauce thickens. Season to taste with salt, pepper and cayenne. Spoon the corn sauce onto 4 heated serving plates and top each with a piece of cooked chicken. Garnish with fresh thyme. Accompany with pureed or baked potatoes and spinach or bitter greens. Serves 4.

Caribbean Chicken

Creamy Bean and Chicken Daube

Creamy Chicken and Bean Daube

Preparation Time: 15 minutes
Cooking Time: 45 minutes

4 chicken legs
salt and freshly ground black pepper
2 tbsp clarified butter
1 tbsp flour
100ml white wine
1 cup chicken stock
2 bayleaves
300ml cream
2 Julia Colbasse sausages, sliced, or 80g spicy
    salami, diced
2×440g cans salad beans, drained and rinsed
½ cup chopped parsley
salt and pepper to taste

Season the chicken with salt and pepper. Brown well all over in batches in clarified butter in a large pan or cast-iron casserole. Reserve. Drain off the fat from the pan, add the flour and wine and bring to a fast boil (dish can be prepared ahead to this point). Mix in the stock, bayleaves, cream, and chicken and simmer uncovered for 25–30 minutes over a low heat, turning the chicken occasionally. Mix in the sausage, beans and parsley and simmer a further 10 minutes. The sauce should be quite thick and the chicken cooked through.

If the sauce is still runny (if your saucepan is narrow and deep you won't get quite the same evaporation), lift out the chicken and boil the sauce hard for a few minutes to reduce. Adjust the seasonings to taste. Serves 6. Accompany with herby whipped potato and steamed bok choy. (To make herby whipped potato, allow about 150g potato per serve, boil until tender, drain and mash with fork until fully broken up. Add a big knob of butter, salt and lots of pepper and about 1 teaspoon chopped fresh thyme and whip up with the fork until smooth and fluffy). Serves 4.

Steamed Bok Choy — allow 1 whole head bok choy per person, wash leaves and either leave whole or slice into 2cm lengths. Steam or stir-fry in a wok with a little water. Season lightly with salt and pepper and a small knob of butter or oil.

To Blanch Spinach

Wash the leaves and remove stalks. Pour over boiling water and leave for a few seconds until soft. Rinse with plenty of cold water. Gently squeeze out the excess water with your hands. Transfer to paper towels to dry.

One-Pot Dining

From classics such as coq au vin and chicken pot pie, to lesser known but equally tasty dishes, such as couscous, chicken lends itself extremely well to one-pot dining.

Spicy Chicken Couscous with Roasted Peppers and Fresh Green Beans

This stunning couscous comes from renowned cook and entertainer Lauraine Jacobs. It's a great recipe for entertaining, as most of it can be prepared ahead.

Preparation Time: 30 minutes
plus 45 minutes marinating/soaking
Cooking Time: 40 minutes

12 chicken pieces or single boneless breasts
¼ cup olive oil
1 tsp each of ground cumin and coriander
pinch of chilli
salt and pepper
juice and finely grated rind of 1 lemon
250g couscous
about 8 cups well-seasoned chicken stock
good pinch saffron threads
1 small onion, finely diced
2 tsp crushed garlic
400g tin tomatoes in juice
garnish: flesh of 2 red and 2 yellow peppers roasted
400g tender young green beans, blanched
¼ cup chopped fresh coriander and/or mint

Marinate the chicken with the olive oil, spices, and the lemon juice and rind for 30 minutes. Soak the couscous in a bowl with 3 cups of the stock, and leave for at least 45 minutes, adding some water if the couscous will absorb it. In a cup soak the saffron with a little warm water. Heat a large pan and brown the chicken in batches, reserving to one side. Add the onion and garlic and cook gently until softened. Add the remaining stock, tomatoes and juice and saffron. Bring to a simmer and cook until the chicken is tender. Adjust the seasonings to taste. To heat the couscous, place in a steamer lined with a muslin cloth and steam until heated through (about 10 minutes) or microwave for 5 minutes in a covered bowl. While the chicken cooks, blanch the beans for 1 minute. Drain and cool in cold water. Just before serving, mix the roasted peppers and blanched beans into the chicken. Simmer for 5 minutes. Tip the couscous onto a large platter, place the chicken on top with the vegetables, spoon over any sauce and scatter over coriander or mint. Serve at once. Serves 8–10.

Menu

One-Pot Celebratory Dinner for Six

Whitebait fritters

Crostini with roasted peppers, tapenade and anchovies

Spicy Chicken Couscous

Lemon Honey and Raspberry Flan

Preparation
1 Prepare crostini bases and toppings
2 Prepare flan base and lemon honey
3 Prepare ingredients for couscous
4 Make whitebait fritters
5 Cook couscous, assemble crostini

Suggested Wines
New Zealand methode champenoise to start, Shiraz or Cabernet Sauvignon with the couscous, chilled dessert wine eg botrysised riesling for the dessert

---

Harvest Chicken Pot Pie

Everyone loves the thyme-flavoured scone dough that tops this rustic chicken pie.

Preparation Time: 20 minutes
Cooking Time: 30–40 minutes

Topping
2 cups self-raising flour
½ tsp salt
1 ½ tbsp fresh chopped rosemary
¾ cup milk
¼ cup oil
2 tbsp butter
800g boneless, skinless chicken, diced in 3cm pieces
2 onions, diced
2 cloves garlic, crushed
1 tsp mild curry powder
2 stalks celery, sliced
2 carrots, peeled and sliced
optional: 1 red pepper, sliced
400g mushrooms, sliced
1 tsp each of chopped rosemary, tarragon and dried basil
2 bayleaves

Harvest Chicken Pot Pie (top); Spicy Chicken Couscous

440g tin mushroom soup
½ cup white wine
½ cup water

Prepare the scone topping first. Mix the self-raising flour, salt and rosemary in a bowl. Combine the milk and oil. Make a well in the dry ingredients and mix in the liquid quickly to form a softish dough. Chill while preparing the chicken filling. Heat the butter in a heavy pan and quickly brown the chicken, half at a time. Transfer to a casserole. Add the onion, garlic, curry powder, celery, carrot and optional pepper to the pan and cook until tender. Add the mushrooms and herbs, increase the heat and cook until the pan is dry. Add the mushroom soup, wine and water and bring to a simmer. Pour over the chicken and mix through evenly. (Dish can be prepared ahead to this point and chilled until required.) Roll the scone dough on a lightly floured board to fit the top of the casserole dish. Arrange the dough on top of the casserole to form a sealed cover, crimping the edges with a fork. Slash the dough with a sharp knife to form a diamond pattern. Brush with a little milk and bake at 200°C for 30–40 minutes. Serves 6. If preferred, individual scones can be cooked separately on a baking tray. The casserole can also be topped with puff pastry, in which case bake at 200°C for 10 minutes, then reduce the heat to 180°C and cook a further 20–30 minutes.

Italian Pot Roasted Chicken with Garlic and Herbs

Rich with the flavours of garlic and herbs, this easy ovenbake makes a great cook-ahead dinner accompanied with Tuscan Cheese Bake (see page 106).

Preparation Time: 15 minutes
Cooking Time: 30–35 minutes

1 tbsp oil, preferably olive
6 chicken pieces (or 1 whole chicken, cut into pieces)
3 whole heads garlic, halved horizontally
2 tsp each of dried rosemary and oregano
salt and lots of freshly ground pepper
1 cup dry white wine
optional: 2 tbsp grated parmesan cheese

Heat the oil in a large, heavy casserole and brown the chicken pieces in batches well all over. Drain off the oil and return the chicken to the pan with the halved heads of garlic, rosemary, oregano, salt, pepper and wine. Cover and bake at 180°C for about 30–35 minutes, or until the chicken is tender, turning the chicken pieces and garlic twice during cooking. If the liquid dries up, add a little water or wine. Pour the juices over the chicken when serving, then sprinkle over optional parmesan cheese. Serves 4–6.

Coq Au Vin

This traditional french chicken casserole is a well-loved favourite. If you are planning to serve it for a party, try using poussin halves in place of the drumsticks.

Preparation Time: 15 minutes
Cooking Time: approximately 1 hour

2 tbsp clarified butter
8–10 chicken drumsticks
10–12 baby onions, or 3 medium onions cut into
  wedges
3 rashers bacon, diced
2 small carrots, diced
1 large parsnip, diced
2–3 heads garlic, cut in half crosswise
2 tbsp brandy
2 cups red wine
2 cups chicken stock
4 bayleaves
3 sprigs fresh marjoram or thyme
salt and freshly ground black pepper
1 tbsp arrowroot or cornflour, mixed to a paste with
  a little water

Heat half the butter in a heavy pan and brown the drumsticks well all over, transferring them to a large casserole as they brown. Add the remaining butter and saute the onion, bacon, carrots, parsnip and garlic over a low heat for about 10 minutes. Add the brandy and ignite, then add the wine and stock and simmer for 5 minutes. Transfer to the casserole dish, adding the herbs and seasonings. Bake, tightly covered for 45 minutes at 180°C without disturbing. Remove the chicken pieces from the dish and thicken the juices with the arrowroot paste, adjusting the seasonings to taste. When the sauce is thickened, return the chicken to heat through. Accompany with crisp cooked vegetables and crusty french bread or a potato gratin. Serves 6.

How to Butterfly a Bird

Using kitchen scissors cut on either side of the bird's backbone, remove the backbone (save for the stockpot). Turn the bird over so it sits breast upwards on the bench. Press the breasts to flatten out the bird as much as possible. Once cooked, the bird is best portioned by cutting the thighs from the breast and cutting the breast into two pieces.

Fast Roasting Techniques

With its crisp golden skin and juicy flesh, roasted chicken is an all-time favourite.
A brief burst in the microwave before roasting speeds up the process
considerably and seems to keep the
bird moist.

Fast-Track Roast Chicken and Vegetables

Preparation Time: 10 minutes
Cooking Time: 22–27 minutes

No 8 chicken, butterflied flat
6 tbsp lemon juice
2 tbsp fresh rosemary or 2 tsp dried
rock salt and pepper
about 1kg root vegetables, eg kumara, potatoes,
  pumpkin, etc, cleaned and cut in 4cm chunks
2 bulbs garlic
2 tbsp olive oil

Preheat the oven to 220°C. Wipe the opened-out chicken dry with a paper towel, then sprinkle both sides with lemon juice, rosemary, salt and pepper. Place in a microwave dish, cover and cook for about 10–12 minutes on high, until juices run semi-clear when pricked in the inner thigh. Cook the root vegetables in a pot of boiling water for 5 minutes. Drain thoroughly and cool on a tray. Break the garlic heads into separate cloves. Mix the vegetables and garlic in oil, and season with salt and pepper. Place the chicken in a large roasting dish, surround with the par-cooked oiled vegetables and bake at 220°C for 12–15 minutes until both chicken and vegetables are golden and cooked through. Cut the bird into 4–6 portions to serve. Serves 4–6.

Fast Track Roast Chicken and Vegetables

Tandoori Roasted Chicken

Marinating the chicken in an Indian Tandoori marinade, then applying the quick-roasting technique, delivers a similar effect to the traditional tandoor — the flesh is moist and juicy and the skin crusty and dark.

Preparation Time: 10 minutes plus marinating
Cooking Time: 20 minutes

Marinade
½ cup unsweetened natural yoghurt
1 small onion, grated
2 tsp crushed garlic
grated rind and juice of 1 lemon
1 tsp each of paprika, garam masala, ground cumin
½ tsp each of ground ginger, chilli powder, salt and
  black pepper

No 6 chicken, butterflied flat (see box at left)

Combine the marinade ingredients and brush both sides of the chicken, pouring over any extra marinade. Allow to marinate for at least 2 hours. Put in a shallow dish, cover tightly and microwave on 100% power for 8 minutes, turning after 4 minutes. Transfer to a pre-heated 220°C oven and cook a further 10 minutes until crisp and golden. Serves 4–5.

Menu

A Mid Week Roast

Fast-Track Roast Chicken and Vegetables

Stir-fried Vegetables

Banana and Coconut Parcels with Spiced Sugar

Preparation
1 Prepare Banana and Coconut Parcels with Spiced
  Sugar
2 Prepare and cook Chicken and Vegetables
3 Prepare and cook Stir-fried Vegetables
4 Cook Banana and Coconut Parcels after Chicken
  and Vegetables are cooked.

Suggested Wine
Chardonnay

Meat

The days of plates piled high with meat and little more, a legacy of our farming forebears, have all but disappeared. Increasingly, for reasons of both health and economy, we are choosing to eat less meat, choosing more meat-free meals and seeking quick strategies with lean cuts that provide maximum results for minimum effort. Lean meat is an excellent source of high-quality protein and today's tailored cuts allow for great results in minutes. Slow-cooking cuts needn't be left out of the busy cook's repertoire. Often the preparation they require is minimal, and the taste of good old-fashioned comfort fare can't be matched.

Black Bean and Chilli Beef Noodles ; Mexican Lamb Fajitas; Pork fillets with Tomato Honey Glaze

Dinner in a Dish

Quick cooking, tender steak cuts are always a popular choice among meat lovers. But steak isn't just about steak and onions or mushrooms. Today's steak plates often see these cuts extended in one-dish creations with starches and vegetables to provide light, well-balanced meals. It's a nutritious formula that looks and tastes great with little effort.

Mexican Lamb or Beef Fajitas

With a jar of spice mix, you can whip up tasty Mexican-style stir-fries and steaks. I prefer to make up a big jar of my own, but Paul Prudhommes Cajun Spice Mix is a good substitute. As well as using on whole pieces of meat, it can be tossed through strips of schnitzel or steak for a barbecue or stir-fry.

Preparation Time: 10 minutes plus marinating
Cooking Time: 10 minutes plus standing

2–3 tbsp fajita spice mix (see page 9)
1 tbsp oil
500g lamb rump, beef fillet or rump in the piece
2 medium onions, halved and cut in thin wedges
1–2 green or red peppers, cut into thin strips
4 potatoes, cut in thin wedges
2 tbsp oil
optional: 1–2 tbsp sweet chilli sauce
garnish: chopped coriander or mint

Combine the spice mix and oil and rub all over the meat. Leave to marinate for at least 1 hour (or up to 24 hours in the fridge). Lightly oil a heavy pan or barbecue plate and brown the meat all over on a high heat. Mix the vegetables with the second quantity of oil and optional chilli sauce and add to the pan. Reduce the heat to medium and cook until the meat is done and the vegetables are cooked and lightly browned. Stand the meat for 5 minutes before carving. Garnish with chopped coriander or mint. Serve with cooked peppers and onions, a salsa of your choice and tortillas. Accompany with a bowl of sour cream and guacamole.

Black Bean and Chilli Beef Noodles

This great dish transforms a couple of steaks into a wonderful platter of spicy flavours.

Preparation Time: 10 minutes plus marinating
Cooking Time: 10–12 minutes

2 large (300–400g) frying steaks, or 2 pork fillets
1 tsp crushed garlic
1 tbsp black bean sauce
1–2 tsp chilli sauce (to taste)
2 tbsp oil
300g egg noodles
2 tbsp sesame oil
½ tsp crushed garlic
2 tsp soy sauce
2 spring onions, sliced
½ cup toasted peanuts
½–1 red pepper, sliced
200g beans, blanched
garnish: 2 tbsp toasted sesame seeds

Mix the meat with the garlic, bean sauce, chilli sauce and oil. Leave to marinate for 15–30 minutes. Cook the noodles. Cook the steaks to medium-rare or pan-fry the pork fillets until cooked. Combine the sesame oil, garlic and soy sauce and toss through the drained noodles. Mix in all the other ingredients. Pile onto a platter. Slice the meat thinly and arrange over the top. Garnish with sesame seeds. Serves 4.

Pork Fillets with Tomato Honey Glaze

This quick, light glaze, using tender pork fillets, makes a stylish meal in minutes. Take care not to overcook the pork, it should be moist with just pink juices when carved.

Preparation Time: 5 minutes
Cooking Time: 10 minutes

1 tbsp tomato paste
2 tbsp honey
1 tsp fresh thyme leaves
pinch each of salt and pepper
2 tsp malt vinegar
2 pork fillets
optional garnish: strips of red pepper

Place the tomato paste, honey, thyme, salt, pepper and vinegar in a microwave jug or small saucepan. Cook on 100% power for 2 minutes until thick and bubbling. Place the fillets on a microwave plate and spread over the paste. Microwave for 5 minutes, then remove and press in the thickest part — the meat should feel

Pan-Fried Beef Steaks with Vegetable Chilli

medium-firm without much give. If it is still very soft, return to the microwave for a further minute. Stand for 5 minutes before carving. The meat should be very slightly pink. Alternatively, cook the fillets in a pan over a low heat for 8–10 minutes until cooked through. Slice slightly on the diagonal in thin slices. Serve on crispy kumara cakes (see page 112), with lightly cooked Chinese greens. Serves 4–5.

Pan-fried Beef Steaks with Vegetable Chilli

The vegetable chilli for this meal can be cooked a day or two in advance and left in the fridge.

Preparation Time: 5 minutes
Cooking Time: 15 minutes

1 tbsp oil
1 tsp crushed garlic
½–1 tsp chilli powder
1 tbsp tomato paste
about 600g diced or sliced vegetables, eg 1 egg-
*   plant, 2–3 zucchini, 1 red or green pepper, 200g*
*   green beans*
400g tin tomatoes in juice
2 tsp chopped fresh rosemary

1 tbsp chopped fresh oregano or 2 tsp dried
salt, pepper and a pinch of sugar
4–6 lean frying steaks

Heat the oil in a saucepan and cook the garlic, chilli powder and tomato paste for a minute. Add all the other ingredients. Cover tightly and cook for 5 minutes, stirring occasionally. Cook the steaks to your preferred doneness. Spoon a pile of hot vegetable chilli onto each serving plate and top with a cooked steak. Serves 4–6.

Chilli

Chilli powder can be anything from pure dried chillies to a blend of dried chillies, red peppers, oregano, cumin and garlic powder. Test the brand for hotness and adjust recipes to suit your taste. Chilli sauce is also incredibly varied — Thai chilli sauces have excellent flavour. The Thai sweet chilli sauce, with seeds in it, is a great all-purpose sauce. Freeze fresh chillies for anytime use. Each variety differs in heat and flavour — as a general rule of thumb the smaller the chilli, the hotter it will be.

Menu

Mid-week Winter Dinner on the Run

China Coast Beef and Noodles
Spiced Apple and Berry Crumble

Preparation
1 Prepare ingredients for main course and cook noodles
2 Prepare crumble and cook
3 Cook stir fry

Suggested wine
Fumé blanc

Ginger Pork and Broccoli

The fresh ginger in this easy stir-fry gives it a real lift. Beef or chicken are also delicious prepared this way.

Preparation Time: 10 minutes
Cooking Time: 10 minutes

400g pork or beef steaks
cornflour for coating
300g broccoli, cut into florets, blanched for 2 minutes
2 tbsp oil
2 tsp honey
2 tbsp soy sauce
2 tsp root ginger, finely chopped
1/4 tsp chilli powder
2 tsp crushed garlic
1/4 cup rice wine or 2 tbsp sherry
3 spring onions
1/4 cup toasted cashew nuts or sunflower seeds

Cut the meat into thin strips and shake lightly in cornflour. Blanch the broccoli. Heat the oil in a wok or large frying-pan, add the meat and stir-fry in batches over a high heat until browned. Return all the meat to the pan and add the honey, soy sauce, ginger, chilli powder and garlic. Stir well. Add the rice wine or sherry, broccoli, spring onions and toasted nuts. Toss to combine. Serve immediately with rice or noodles. Serves 4.

China Coast Beef and Noodles

Preparation Time: 10 minutes
Cooking Time: 15 minutes

2 large onions, cut in thin segments
1 tbsp sesame oil
1 tsp crushed garlic
1/2 cup water
1/2 cup oyster sauce
1 tsp hot chilli sauce
salt and freshly ground black pepper
1 tbsp oil
400g rump or sirloin steak, or schnitzel, thinly sliced
300–400g sliced vegetables, eg red or green peppers, beans, carrots and snowpeas

In a wok or large pan, cook the onions in the oil until clear. Add the garlic and cook for another minute. Add the water, oyster and chilli sauces and simmer for 5 minutes. Season to taste. Reserve until ready to use. Slice the meat thinly across the grain. Blanch the vegetables in boiling water for 1 minute. Drain and cool in cold water. Preheat a heavy pan with a little oil and cook handfuls of beef over a high heat for about 40 seconds on each side to seal. Add the meat to the hot sauce with the blanched vegetables and allow to heat through. Serve with noodles or rice. Serves 4–5.

To prepare egg noodles, allow about 60–75g per person. Cook in plenty of boiling salted water according to manufacturer's instructions.

Texas Chilli

Recipes for chilli abound — enough to fill entire volumes. Everyone has their own version of what's good and what's hot. This one's good — I'll leave the hotness up to you. If you wish to extend the recipe, add a can of rinsed, drained kidney beans.

Preparation Time: 20 minutes
Cooking Time: 30 minutes

3 tbsp cooking oil
750g lean beef mince
salt and pepper
2 tbsp tomato paste
2 tsp crushed garlic
1 tsp each of dried red pepper flakes and oregano
1–2 tsp chilli powder (to taste)
1/2 red pepper, finely diced
400g tin tomatoes in juice, pureed
2 cups beef stock
optional: 1/2 cup taco sauce
2 cups whole kernel corn
1/2 cup pitted green olives, sliced

Heat the oil in a large frypan. Season the mince with salt and pepper and brown well over a high heat. Add the tomato paste, garlic, pepper flakes, oregano and chilli powder and cook a further minute. Add the peppers, tomatoes and stock. Simmer for 30 minutes. Mix in optional Taco sauce, corn and olives and adjust the seasoning to taste. Serves 6. Accompany with rice and hot pepper sauce.

China Coast Beef and Noodles

Texas Chilli

Lamb and Beans with Indian Spices

Lamb combines well with both Indian and Mexican spices. Lean lamb steaks make a good choice for tasty quick curries like this one.

Preparation Time: 15 minutes plus marinating
Cooking Time: 15 minutes

400g lean lamb steaks
1 tbsp ground cumin
1 tsp each of mild curry powder and paprika
¼ tsp each of ground cloves, cinnamon and cayenne pepper
2 tbsp oil
1 large onion, finely sliced
2 tsp crushed garlic
1 cup beef stock (or ½ cup canned beef broth, mixed to 1 cup with water)
2 tbsp sultanas
1 tsp cornflour, mixed with 1 tbsp water
salt
300g green beans, blanched for 1 minute in boiling water

Cut the meat into thin strips. Place in a bowl and mix through all the spices with 1 tbsp of the oil. Marinate for at least 15 minutes or for 2–3 hours in the fridge.

Brown the meat in batches over a high heat (approx 5 minutes). Set aside. Heat the remaining oil and cook the onion until tender. Add the garlic and cook a further minute. Add the stock, sultanas and meat and simmer over a low heat for 10 minutes. Five minutes before serving, add the beans. Thicken with cornflour paste and adjust the seasonings to taste. Serves 4.

Stir-frying Technique for Meat Dishes

- Choose lean cuts
- Slice the meat thinly across the grain
- Slice vegetables as required before commencing cooking
- Marinate as desired, draining meat from marinade before cooking
- Cook in small batches over high heat to prevent overcrowding, which will cause the meat to form juices and become dry
- Semi-cook vegetables separately and add at the end
- Eat immediately and don't attempt to reheat

Super Steak Saucery

Steak and onions, steak and mushrooms, steak with creamy peppercorn sauce. Whatever the sauce, a good steak is a favourite choice for meat lover's. Choose lean, well-aged steak cuts and take care not to overcook.

Steaks with Green Peppercorn Sauce

Argentina is famous for its beef and its tender, juicy steaks. I discovered this method of cooking them in a wonderful restaurant in Bariloche a few years back. The technique of finishing steak in the sauce makes the meat very juicy and tender.

Preparation Time: 10 minutes
Cooking Time: 20 minutes

1 tbsp butter
1 tbsp shallots, finely diced
200ml red wine
4 cups good beef or venison stock
3 tbsp green peppercorns
pinch cinnamon
1 tsp finely grated lemon rind
2 tsp wine vinegar
2 tsp arrowroot or cornflour, mixed with a ¼ cup port
6 beef or venison steaks
a little butter to cook
garnish: wedges of lemon, sprigs of oregano

To prepare the sauce, heat the butter in a large frypan and cook the shallots until softened. Add the wine to the pan and bring to a fast boil. Add the stock and boil hard until the mixture has reduced to about 2 cups total (about 15 minutes). Add the peppercorns, cinnamon, lemon rind and wine vinegar and simmer for 5 minutes. Mix in the cornflour and port paste and stir until lightly thickened. Adjust the seasonings to taste. When ready to serve, brown the steaks well in a preheated pan for about 2 minutes. Add the prepared sauce to the meat pan and simmer at the lowest possible heat for 2–3 minutes just until the meat is medium-rare. Lift the meat from the sauce and slice thinly. Arrange in a fan pattern on the plate and spoon over a little sauce. Garnish with the lemon rind and oregano. Serves 6.

Pan-fried Cervena Venison with Tapenade and Peppers

Cervena venison is extremely tender and lean. It needs no ageing or marinating but can easily be overcooked. Never cook Cervena beyond medium-rare or you will be disappointed with a dry, tough result.

Preparation Time: 5 minutes
Cooking Time: 3 minutes

1 tbsp olive oil
6 venison steaks, cut 2cm thick (or 6 beef steaks)
freshly ground black pepper
1 red pepper, cut in thin strips and lightly sauteed
¼ cup prepared tapenade (see page 9)
garnish: black olives and fresh herbs, eg oregano, basil or mint

Heat a heavy pan with the oil until it shimmers. Fry the red pepper until lightly brown and softened. Reserve to one side. Sprinkle the steaks with black pepper and pan-fry over a high heat for 40–60 seconds each side. Place a cooked steak onto each serving plate and top with 2 tsp of olive topping. Top with a lattice of cooked pepper strips. Garnish as desired with olives and fresh herbs. Serves 6.

Beef Nicoise

Schnitzel is a great cut for stir-fries and sautes. Slice it into thin strips and take care not to overcook.

Preparation Time: 15 minutes
Cooking Time: 15 minutes

1 tbsp oil
400g beef schnitzel, cut in 1 cm strips
2 tsp crushed garlic

Cooking the Perfect Steak

- Choose lean, well-aged steak cut 1.5–2cm thick
- Season and cook in a hot pan with a little oil or butter
- For rare steaks allow about 40–50 seconds per side
- For medium-rare steaks allow 1–1½ minutes per side
- For well done allow 2–3 minutes per side
- Stand for 1–2 minutes before serving
- If cooking steaks thicker than 2cm, brown first in a pan then finish in a 220°C oven for 4–6 minutes.

Beef Nicoise

1 tbsp tapenade (see page 9)
1 tsp dried oregano
400g tin tomatoes in juice, pureed
400g fresh beans, cut into chunks and blanched
½ cup black olives
salt and freshly ground black pepper

Heat the oil in a large frypan. Brown the meat over a high heat in batches and set aside. Add the garlic, tapenade and oregano and cook for 30 seconds. Add the tomatoes and simmer for 10 minutes. Add the beans and simmer for 3 minutes. Add the cooked meat and olives and simmer for 1 minute. Season to taste with salt and pepper and serve. Serves 4.

Hungarian Pepper and Beef Goulash

Caraway seeds have a nuttiness that Hungarians adore. Red peppers, paprika and garlic combine with caraway in the rich, meaty sauce of this great pan saute.

Preparation Time: 5 minutes
Cooking Time: 15 minutes

1 tbsp oil
1 large onion, finely diced
2 large red peppers, finely diced
2 tsp paprika
optional: 1 tsp caraway seeds
2 tsp crushed garlic
2 tbsp tomato paste
2 cups beef stock (or 1 can beef broth thinned with
    2 cups water)
400g rump steak or schnitzel, cut into thin strips
salt and pepper to taste
½ cup light sour cream
¼ cup parsley, finely chopped

Heat the oil and cook the onion, pepper, paprika and optional caraway seeds until the onion is soft. Add the garlic and tomato paste to the pan and cook, stirring over heat, for a further minute. Add the stock and simmer for 5–7 minutes. Reduce the heat to very low and add the meat. Cover and cook on the lowest heat for 5 minutes. Do not allow to boil or the meat will be tough. Remove from the heat, season with salt and pepper and mix in the sour cream and parsley. Serves 4–5. Accompany with noodles or baked potatoes and lightly cooked vegetables or salad.

Quick Roasts with Lamb Racks

Lamb Racks with Kiwifruit Dipping Sauce

Sweet, tender lamb racks flash-roasted and served with a fresh fruit salsa make a great offering for a casual dinner party. Get the butcher to trim and chine them for you.

Preparation Time: 10 minutes
Cooking Time: 12–15 minutes

2 lamb racks, chined and trimmed of fat
salt and freshly ground black pepper
1 recipe Kiwifruit and Pawpaw Salsa (see page 64)

Season the lamb and roast at 220°C for 12–15 minutes until medium-rare. Stand for 10 minutes before carving. Carve the racks and accompany with the salsa.
Serves 6.

Honey Mustard Crust for Lamb Racks

¼ cup coarse mustard
2 tbsp runny honey
1 tbsp fresh chopped rosemary

Combine all the ingredients and coat the fleshy part of the lamb racks. Makes enough for 2 lamb racks. Roast as above in lamb racks with kiwi salsa.

The Press Test for Doneness

Ascertaining the doneness of a roast of meat or a steak can easily be done by comparing the texture of the flesh on your palm at the base of your thumb with that of the meat you are cooking.

Rare: completely relax your hand and press the fleshy area of your palm at base of your thumb. If the meat feels very soft and loose like this, then it is very rare.

Medium-rare: hold your palm flat and and press the fleshy area of your palm at base of your thumb. If the meat feels quite bouncy like this, then it is cooked to medium-rare.

Well-done: stretch your palm back as far as you can and press the fleshy area of your palm at base of your thumb. If the meat has very little give and or quite rigid like this, then it is is cooked to well-done.

Rack of Lamb with Minted Zucchini Stuffing

This recipe may sound a bit complicated, but it's actually quite simple. Once you have formed a pocket in the rack, it can be stuffed with anything — sundried tomatoes and prunes, spinach and bacon or this tasty mixture of zucchini and basil that looks so pretty when you slice the racks. Stuffed racks can be prepared ahead and kept in the fridge until they are ready to be cooked.

Preparation Time: approx 15 minutes
Cooking Time: 12–15 minutes

4 small zucchini, cut in matchsticks
1 tsp butter
1 tsp crushed garlic
1 tbsp basil or herb pesto (or 2 tbsp chopped fresh herbs)
2 racks of lamb, chined and excess fat removed
salt and black pepper to taste

Crust

2 tbsp Dijon mustard
1 ½ tbsp fresh chopped rosemary

Microwave the zucchini with the butter, garlic and basil for 2 minutes on 100% power or cook in a saucepan until just crisp but tender. Cool. Using a sharp thin-bladed knife make a pocket through the eye of the rack, taking care not to poke the knife through the sides. Carefully stuff the zucchini matchsticks into the pocket. Place in a roasting dish, spread the mustard over the top surface of the rack and sprinkle with rosemary. Roast at 220°C for 12–15 minutes until medium rare Stand for 5–6 minutes before carving. Serves 5–6.

Berry Sauce for Lamb, Beef or Venison

In a saucepan, heat 3 tbsp brown sugar and ¼ cup malt vinegar for about 2 minutes until they form a pale caramel. Add 2 cups frozen raspberries and simmer over low heat for about 15 minutes. Strain through a fine sieve to remove the pips. Mix in 2 tsp cornflour and combine with 1 tbsp port and stir until the sauce is lightly thickened. Season to taste. Makes about 2 cups.

90s Roast Meat and Vegetables

Many people believe roasts require a lot of fat to cook properly. They don't. What they do need is high heat and a decent period of standing once cooked so the

juices can disperse evenly. If you are dealing with a tougher cut, such as shoulder, cook it with some water in a covered dish for the first 1½ hours of cooking to semi-steam the meat, then finish it in a hot oven to crisp the skin. Again don't forget to stand it.

Preparation Time: 20 minutes
Cooking Time: 40 minutes

800g–1kg piece lean beef or lamb, eg lamb leg, beef sirloin, beef fillet (or a bigger cut)
optional crust: 2 tbsp mustard, 1 tbsp honey, 1 tbsp tomato sauce
4–6 small onions, in the skin
2–3 whole heads garlic, halved crosswise
4–6 medium potatoes, scrubbed and cut in 4cm cubes
¼–½ pumpkin, washed and cut into chunks
2–3 large kumara, scrubbed and cut into chunks
optional: 2 red peppers, seeds and pith removed, cut in quarters
2 tbsp oil
1 tbsp chopped fresh rosemary

Preheat the oven to 220°C. Trim the fat from the meat, fold under any thin edges and tie to secure. Place the meat in a roasting tray. Combine the mustard, honey and tomato sauce and spread over the top and sides of the meat. Prepare the vegetables. Drop the prepared root vegetables and baby onions into a saucepan of boiling water and boil for 5 minutes. Drain thoroughly. Roast the meat at 220°C for 10 minutes. Reduce the heat to 200°C and cook another 30 minutes. At this time add the par-cooked root vegetables and garlic. After 15 minutes add the optional peppers and cook for the remaining 15 minutes until all vegetables are cooked. Take out the meat and leave to rest on the bench. Increase the oven temperature to 220°C and crisp the vegetables for a further 5–10 minutes. Carve the meat in thin slices, overlap on a large platter and surround with root vegetables. Serves 4–6. Accompany with lightly cooked vegetables.

To make a gravy: remove the meat and vegetables from the roasting pan. Put the vegetables onto an oven-proof plate and return to a 220°C oven to crisp. Drain off all but 1 tbsp of fat from pan, retaining the pan drippings. Heat the pan on an element. Add 2 cups stock or vegetable water, 1 tsp minced fresh thyme and thicken with 2 tbsp cornflour or arrowroot mixed with ¼ cup port or red wine. Simmer for 5–10 minutes to cook out the flour and evaporate the alcohol. Season to taste and serve in a jug. Makes 2 cups, enough for 6–8 servings.

Lamb Chwarma Pockets

No need to call for takeouts next time you fancy a Middle Eastern feast. These pita pockets filled with Middle Eastern-style lamb are scrumptious. Use this great marinade for any of your summer lamb barbecues.

Preparation Time: 5–10 minutes
Cooking Time: 10 minutes

500g lean lamb, cut into tiny slivers
1 tsp each of ground cumin, dried oregano, allspice
¼ tsp cinnamon
1 medium onion, finely diced
2 tsp crushed garlic
1 tbsp olive oil
salt and freshly ground black pepper
juice of 1 lemon

Accompaniments

pita breads
parsley and sprout salad
garlic and chive sour cream
spiked tomato relish

Combine the lamb with the spices, onion, garlic and oil. Leave for at least 15 minutes before cooking, or up to 6 hours refrigerated. Preheat a pan or barbecue hotplate to medium-high and oil lightly. Cook the lamb, tossing over heat for 3–4 minutes, until it is just browned. Season to taste with salt and pepper. Place the meat in a serving dish and keep warm. Squeeze over the lemon juice. Serve the meat with warmed pita pockets and accompaniments. Serves 4–6.

*To prepare warmed pita pockets, slice the pita breads in half. Stack one half on top of the other and wrap in tinfoil. Place on a hot barbecue or oven and turn the tinfoil frequently until warmed through (5–10 minutes).

Lamb Chwarma Pockets

Menu

Al Fresco Holiday Lunch

Platter of Fritters, Olives and Garlic Pita Crisps
*Lamb Chwarmas with Pita Bread
and Accompaniments*
Greek Salad
Summer Stonefruit Clafoutis

Preparation
1 Prepare fritters and pita crisps
2 Marinate lamb for chwarmas and prepare accompaniments
3 Make Greek Salad
4 Prepare dessert

Suggested wine
Chilled Pinot Noir

Spicy Tomato Spare Ribs

Tender ribs in a spicy Mexican-flavoured sauce just melt in your mouth. Be sure to buy short meaty ribs.

Preparation Time: 10 minutes
Cooking Time: 65 minutes

1.5kg pork spare ribs

Marinade

2 tbsp each of tomato paste and honey
1 cup orange juice
1 tsp each of crushed garlic, ground cumin, ground ginger, dried oregano, and mustard
1 tbsp sweet chilli sauce

Cut the ribs into serving pieces (about 2–3 ribs wide) and place in a roasting pan. Combine the remaining ingredients and pour over. Cover and bake for 35 minutes at 170°C, then remove the cover and bake, turning every 5 minutes, for a further 30 minutes or until ribs are glazed. Serves 6–8.

Gourmet Burgers
90s Beef Burger Combinations

- Bacon, avocado, spinach, mayonnaise and roasted red pepper
- Tapenade, sliced gruyere cheese, tomato and red pepper
- Fried onions, banana, mayonnaise and shredded spinach
- Beetroot, shredded lettuce, tomato and egg

Mediterranean Summer Grill Plate

This recipe is a great formula for a summer barbecue or terrace dinner with friends. The meat cooks in a whole piece for about 40–45 minutes with the vegetables added in the last 30 minutes. The result presents beautifully and makes a great meal-in-one. A variety of meat and venison cuts can be used. The thicker the cut, the longer the cook time — a sirloin will take 10–15 minutes longer than the thinner venison rump.

Preparation Time: 15 minutes
Cooking Time: about 20 minutes

1–1.2kg piece beef fillet, sirloin, flank steak or
* Cervena venison — 5–6cm thick*
½ cup olive oil
2 large cloves garlic, crushed
½ tsp finely grated lemon rind
2 tbsp lemon juice
1 tbsp chopped fresh rosemary
black pepper
Vegetables (see below for a selection) use any
* combination of 4–5 per person*

Mediterranean Summer Grill Plate

Trim the meat to an even-sized piece, folding in any thin edges and secure with string. Place in a clean plastic bag or dish. Combine the oil and garlic and pour half over the meat. Sprinkle over lemon rind and juice and rosemary and marinate for at least 30 minutes or up to 12 hours in the fridge. Reserve the rest of the garlic-flavoured oil for the vegetables.

Vegetable Preparations

Artichokes: drop into a big saucepan of water with the juice of 1 lemon and boil for 10 minutes. Drain, cool and split in half lengthwise. Scoop out the hairy choke, peel the tough outer skin off the stalks and brush all over with garlic oil.

Potatoes: quarter the potato and boil for 5 minutes.

Zucchini or Beans: cut the zucchini into long diagonal slices or leave the beans whole. Blanch the green vegetables for 1 minute in a large saucepan of boiling water, then cool under cold water and drain.

Mushrooms: wipe the mushrooms with a damp cloth, peeling and trimming stalks if necessary.

Peppers: cut into fat strips removing the pith and seeds.

Olives: drain the olives from the brine. Cut in half.

Sweetcorn and Carrots: cut the sweetcorn into 5cm rings and blanch, along with the carrots.

Eggplant: Slice 1½–2cm thick, brush either side with oil.

Garlic: cut the garlic in half horizontally.

Onion: Peel and blanch the onion.

(All of this can be done well in advance if required.)

When ready to cook, preheat a barbecue plate or grill. Lift the meat from its marinade and place onto the grill. Cook over high heat for about 5 minutes each side, then turn heat down to its medium-low setting (for a charcoal cooker, lift the cooking rack until you can hold your hand at the same level over the heat source for 5 seconds before it feels too hot). Cook for 15–20 minutes. Grill the vegetables, brushing well with garlic oil. They will take about 10 minutes to cook. Stand the meat for 5 minutes before carving. Serves 8–10.

Variations: for Mexican-style grill plate, use 2 tbsp of Fajita Spice Mix (see page) or Paul Prudhomme's Cajun Magic to flavour the oil in place of the garlic, rosemary and lemon used here.

For an Asian emphasis, substitute root ginger for the rosemary and mix through a little oyster sauce just before serving.

Garlic, Basil and Anchovy Dipping Sauce

This yummy sauce makes a great accompaniment to the meat and vegetable platter.

1½ cups homemade mayonnaise, 1 egg yolk, 4 mashed anchovy fillets, 15–20 basil leaves or 2 tsp basil pesto, 1 tbsp capers, 2 cloves crushed garlic. Puree all the ingredients until smooth. Makes 1¾ cups.

Steak, Mushroom and Kidney Pudding; Italian Rabbit with Mint and Pinenuts

Braised Oxtails with Red Chilli Beans

This wonderful recipe comes from my neighbour Janice Sommerville. It's one of the nicest preparations for oxtail that I have come across, and tastes even better if made a day in advance.

Preparation Time: 40 minutes
plus overnight soaking of beans
Cooking Time: 3½–4 hours

3kg oxtails, trimmed
seasoned flour for dredging the oxtails
6 tbsp vegetable oil
2 large onions, finely chopped
1 tbsp crushed garlic
1 tbsp grated, peeled root ginger
⅔ cup firmly packed light brown sugar
1½ cups tomato sauce
3 tbsp Dijon-style mustard
1 cup cider vinegar
¼ cup worcestershire sauce
¼ cup lemon juice
tabasco to taste
cayenne to taste
2×400g cans of Italian tomatoes, drained, reserving juice and chopped
salt and freshly ground black pepper, to season
500g dried red kidney beans, soaked overnight in enough cold water to cover them by 4cm and drained
chopped spring onion greens for garnish

Dredge the oxtails in flour, shaking off the excess. In a large, heavy saucepan heat ¼ cup of the oil over moderately high heat until it is hot, but not smoking.

Brown the oxtails in batches and transfer as they are browned to a plate. Add the remaining oil to the saucepan. Cook the onion, garlic and ginger over moderately low heat, stirring, until the onion is softened. Stir in the brown sugar, tomato sauce, mustard, vinegar, worcestershire sauce, lemon juice, tabasco, cayenne, tomatoes with the reserved juice, and salt and pepper. Simmer the sauce, stirring occasionally for 5 minutes. Add the oxtails and simmer the mixture covered, stirring occasionally for 2½ hours. While the oxtails are cooking, in a large saucepan combine the beans with enough cold water to cover them by 4cm. Bring the liquid to a boil and simmer the beans, covered for 1 hour, or until tender. Drain the beans well and stir them into the oxtail mixture. Simmer the mixture, uncovered, stirring occasionally, for 30 minutes to 1 hour, or until the meat is very tender. Serve it sprinkled with scallion greens. Serves 6–8.

Italian Rabbit with Mint and Pinenuts

The slightly sweet-sour flavour of this wonderful rabbit casserole is classically Italian. It's a great dish for a dinner party as it can be cooked ahead of time and reheated.

Preparation Time: 15 minutes
Cooking Time: 30 minutes

1 large rabbit, jointed
seasoned flour to coat
2 tbsp oil
2 large onions, finely sliced
2 cloves garlic, crushed
2½ cups chicken stock
1 cup white wine
5 tbsp balsamic vinegar
4 tsp honey
¼ cup finely chopped mint leaves
½ cup toasted pinenuts
optional: 2 tsp cornflour mixed with a little water to thicken

Shake the rabbit portions in flour to coat. Heat the oil and brown portions well all over. Remove from the pan and place in a casserole dish. Add the onions to the pan and cook over a low heat until soft. Add the garlic, stock and wine to the pan and bring to a fast boil. Boil for 5 minutes, then add the vinegar and honey and boil another 2–3 minutes. Pour over the rabbit portions. Bake at 180°C for 30 minutes. Reheat as desired, garnishing with mint and pinenuts just before serving. Adjust seasoning to taste. Sauce should not need thickening, but it can be thickened with a paste of 2 teaspoons cornflour mixed with a little water, if you prefer. Serves 4, recipe easily doubles.

Lamb Rumps with Sundried Tomatoes and Prunes

Lean, tender lamb rumps make a great party dish. Here they are richly sauced with Mediterranean flavours of garlic, prunes and sundried tomatoes.

Preparation Time: 15 minutes
Cooking Time: up to 35 minutes

6 trimmed lamb rumps
1 tsp crushed garlic
about 18 pitted prunes
1 red pepper, cut into strips
salt and pepper to season

Sauce

2 tbsp, olive oil
1 large onion, cut in thin strips
2 cloves garlic, crushed
1 cup white wine
2×400g tins tomatoes in juice, chopped
1 tsp sugar
1 tbsp spiced vinegar
12–15 sundried tomato halves
salt and lots of freshly ground black pepper

Lay each lamb rump flat on a board and flatten lightly. Top each with a little crushed garlic, about 3 prunes and 2–3 slices of pepper. Fold the meat over to enclose the filling (peppers will stick out the ends) and secure bundles with string or toothpicks. Heat the oil in a large pan, season the meat with salt and pepper and brown quickly all over. Remove from the pan and reserve. Add the onion to the pan and cook until soft, but not browned. Add the garlic, wine, tomatoes and their juice, sugar, vinegar and sundried tomatoes and bring to a simmer. Return the lamb pieces to sauce and simmer slowly for about 20 minutes, turning frequently. Alternatively, transfer all to a casserole dish, cover and bake for 35 minutes at 180°C. To serve, divide sauce between serving plates, slice each parcel into 3, remove strings and arrange on top of the sauce. Serves 6.

Steak, Mushroom and Kidney Pudding

This recipe is comfort food just like granny used to make. The technique is actually a great way to cook tougher meat — you can use it for any slow-cooking cut. Watch that the pan doesn't boil dry.

Preparation Time: 20 minutes
Cooking Time: 2½ hours

700g blade or chuck steak, diced in 2cm chunks
4 lambs kidneys, cut into pieces

Lamb Rumps with Sundried Tomatoes and Prunes

2 large onions, thinly sliced
200g mushrooms, sliced
1 tsp salt
2 bayleaves
1 tsp each of dried thyme and celery salt
¼ cup chopped fresh herbs (include parsley, oregano, chervil, etc)
2 leeks, diagonally sliced
200g baby carrots, washed
freshly ground black pepper
1 tbsp cornflour, mixed with 3 tbsp sherry, port or water
¼ cup chopped parsley

Place the meat and other ingredients up to and including the fresh herbs in a metal basin, and cover with tinfoil. Place the basin in a large saucepan filled with enough water to reach about half way up the container. Cover the saucepan tightly and cook over medium-low heat for 2 hours, adding more liquid to the pot as necessary. Boil the leeks and carrots for 5 minutes. Twenty minutes before the meat is cooked, remove the bayleaves, stir in the cornflour paste and add the par-cooked leeks and carrots. Season with plenty of freshly ground black pepper and add the parsley. Top with dumplings (see below), cover the pot and cook a further 20 minutes. Serves 5–6.

Dumplings

Place 1 cup flour in a basin and mix in ¼ tsp salt, 2 tsp chopped fresh rosemary, 2 tsp chopped fresh thyme and 2 tsp baking powder. Mix in about ¾ cup milk or enough to form a soft dough. Drop spoonfuls onto the simmering (thickened) stew. Cover tightly and cook a further 20 minutes until dumplings are risen and cooked through.

Vegetarian

The bland beansprout offerings of the late 60s and early 70s put people off vegetarian food for years. It's only quite recently that vegetarian cooking has hit the big time, with a range of meatless offerings that taste and look wonderful. Like many people, our household eats meatless meals three or four times a week, choosing to incorporate vegetarian food in bold, fresh tastes that focus on satisfying carbohydrates.

Most restaurants now serve at least one tasty vegetarian option and, thanks to the growth of ethnic restaurants and overseas travel, we have come to realise that vegetarian food is a lot more than tasteless lentil patties and fake meat meatballs. For reasons of both economy and religion, you find a lot of vegetarian cooking in many of the ethnic cuisines — Indian, Chinese, Middle Eastern, and Mexican all offer a great range of meatless meal options that have great taste appeal.

Spicy Mexican Chick Peas, Herb Pancakes with Chilli Ratatouille; Semolina Tortini with Provencal Bean and Eggplant Sauce

Felafels with Yoghurt Sauce

Chickpeas, split peas or even lentils can be used to make tasty felafels.

Preparation Time: 20 minutes plus soaking
Cooking Time: 30 minutes

300g dried split green peas
1 small onion, finely diced
1 tsp crushed garlic
½–1 tsp chilli powder (to taste)
1 tbsp each ground cumin and lemon juice
1 tsp salt and lots of freshly ground black pepper
¼ cup sesame seeds
oil for shallow frying

Cover the green peas with water and leave to soak for a minimum of 1 hour. Drain, place in a saucepan, bring to the boil and simmer for 15 minutes. Drain and place in a food processor with the onion, garlic, chilli powder,cumin and lemon juice. Process until smooth. Season well and roll into balls. Flatten a little then dip in sesame seeds. Fry on a well greased barbecue plate or pan or shallow fry for 1–2 minutes on either side or until golden brown. Drain on paper towels. Makes 24. Felafels can be prepared in advance and reheated at 180°C for 5–8 minutes.

Serving Suggestions: Accompany with lightly toasted pita pockets, bean sprouts, diced tomatoes, diced cucumber, yoghurt and chilli sauce, or serve on a buffet with barbecued lamb.

Yoghurt Sauce

Combine in a bowl 1 cup unsweetened natural yoghurt, a pinch of chilli powder, 2 tbsp chopped mint, a little salt and plenty of freshly ground black pepper. Spoon over the felafel pockets.

Herb Pancakes with Chilli Ratatouille

A simple pancake batter takes on a new taste with the addition of fresh herbs or spices. Serve flavoured pancakes with curried vegetables, this spicy ratatouille or tasty bean and eggplant sauce featured with the tortini for an easy, nutritious vegetarian meal.

Preparation Time: 15 minutes
Cooking Time: 20 minutes

Pancakes

1 cup flour
1 cup milk
2 eggs
1 tsp baking powder

½ tsp salt
¼ cup freshly chopped soft herbs, eg parsley, oregano, basil, dill
2 tbsp melted butter

Blend all the ingredients, except the butter, to make a smooth batter. Beat in the butter. Lightly grease a heavy pan and cook a ladleful of mixture at a time. Cook over a medium heat, turning as bubbles form. Makes 8 large pancakes, serve 2 per person.

Sauce

1 tbsp oil
1 tsp crushed garlic
1 tbsp chilli sauce
½–1 tsp chilli powder
1 tbsp tomato paste
about 600g diced or sliced vegetables, eg 1 eggplant, 2–3 zucchini, 1 red or green pepper
200g green beans
½ cup black olives
400g tin tomatoes in juice
2 tsp chopped fresh rosemary
2 tsp spiced vinegar
salt, pepper and a pinch of sugar

Heat the oil in a saucepan and cook the garlic, chilli sauce, chilli powder and tomato paste for a minute. Add all the other ingredients. Cover tightly and cook for 10 minutes, stirring occasionally. Serves 4.

Semolina Tortini

This tasty Italian savoury semolina roll is rolled up and pan-fried. Delicious with a range of sauces, it can be prepared well in advance and chilled.

Preparation Time: 10 minutes
Cooking Time: 10 minutes

3 cups milk
2 tbsp butter
finely grated rind of 1 lemon
1 ½ cups semolina
salt and pepper
2 eggs
½ cup grated parmesan cheese
extra grated parmesan cheese for dusting

Bring the milk, butter and rind to the boil. Remove from the heat and stir in the semolina. Put the mixture back on the stove and cook for approximately 3 minutes. Mix in the eggs and parmesan cheese. Season to taste. Once the mixture is totally blended, place on greased tinfoil and roll up into a cylinder. Refrigerate to firm mixture (recipe can be made ahead up to this stage). Cut into 1.5cm slices and fry in a lightly oiled pan until browned on each side. Alternatively, spoon the mixture into a baking dish and bake at 220°C for about 30 minutes until golden. Serves 6.

Provencal Bean and Eggplant Sauce

Serve this tasty sauce with the tortini roll or with herb pancakes for a satisfying vegetarian meal.

Preparation Time: 10 minutes
Cooking Time: 10 minutes

¼ cup olive oil
1 medium eggplant, halved and cut in 2cm thick slices
2 tsp crushed garlic
1 ½ cups prepared pasta sauce
2 tbsp pesto
1 tsp dried oregano
1 can soy, kidney or lima beans, drained and rinsed
salt and pepper

Heat the oil and brown the eggplant on both sides. Add the garlic and cook a further 30 seconds. Mix in all other ingredients and simmer for 5 minutes. Season to taste. Serves 2–3.

Vegetable purees are an excellent way to serve fresh vegetables without having to cook them at the last minute. Purees can be made hours in advance and reheated when needed. Almost any vegetable can be pureed, not just starchy vegetables. Create interesting flavours by combining different vegetables in a puree. Try pears and swedes, carrots and cauliflower, roasted onions and pumpkin, leeks and avocado (add the avocado just before serving).

Dark Rich Mushroom Sauce

Dried mushrooms give this sauce an intense rich flavour.

Preparation Time: 10 minutes plus soaking
Cooking Time: 10–12 minutes

4 dried Chinese mushrooms, soaked in ½ cup port or red wine
1 tbsp oil
400g fresh field mushrooms, sliced thinly
1 tsp crushed garlic
2 cups chicken stock, or 1 can chicken broth thinned with water to make 2 cups
1 tsp arrowroot mixed with a little water or lemon juice
salt and pepper

Soak the dried mushrooms for at least 30 minutes or for 6 minutes on defrost power in the microwave. Cut the soaked mushrooms into fine dice, discarding the stalks. Reserve with their liquid. Heat the oil and cook the fresh mushrooms until the pan is dry and the mushrooms start to brown. Add the garlic and allow to cook for a few seconds, then add the stock, dried mushrooms and their liquid and simmer all for 5 minutes. Thicken with arrowroot paste and adjust seasonings to taste. If desired, stir in a spoonful of cream just before serving. Serves 4 with semolina tortini.

Vegetarian Couscous

Moroccan spices perfume this rich vegetable stew. Serve it with flatbread for a wonderful vegetarian feast. If you can't find couscous use bulghur wheat instead — the flavour is slightly different, but the texture is much the same.

Preparation Time: 20 minutes
Cooking Time: 35 minutes

150g couscous or bulghur wheat
water to soak
1 tbsp oil
1 large onion, finely sliced
1 tsp each of crushed garlic, turmeric, paprika, ginger and fennel seeds
½ tsp chilli powder
¼ tsp each of ground cloves and cinnamon
1 can chickpeas, drained
300g prepared root vegetables, eg parsnips, kumara, carrots
200g legumes, eg broad beans, green beans or peas
400g tin tomatoes in juice, pureed
boiling water
salt and pepper
1 tsp butter

Place the couscous in a bowl and cover with boiling water and a pinch of salt. Stand for 15 minutes, drain well and reserve. While the couscous soaks prepare the sauce. Heat the oil in a large heavy-based pan. Add the onion and cook until beginning to brown. Add the garlic and spices and cook a further minute. Mix in the chickpeas, vegetables, tomatoes and water to cover the mixture (about 2 cups). Bring to the boil and simmer over a low heat for 30 minutes. Season well. After 25 minutes cooking, steam or microwave the couscous to heat through with a knob of butter. Place on a large serving dish and spoon over the vegetables and juices. Serves 4. Recipe doubles easily.

This dish is particularly delicious if the sauce is made 1–2 days ahead and refrigerated for the flavours to develop.

Pies, Tarts and Slices

Tuscan Cheese Bake

This is one of those great recipes that you will come back to again and again. It's easy and very satisfying to eat. I often make it without the spinach and serve it with roasted chicken. Semolina is the busy person's substitute for polenta, which, although delicious, needs long continuous stirring over the stove.

Preparation Time: 10 minutes
Cooking Time: 25–35 minutes

4 cups milk
2 tbsp butter
1 tsp salt
1½ cups semolina
3 eggs, lightly beaten
optional: 2 cups cooked spinach — excess liquid removed
1 cup grated cheese
2–3 tbsp grated parmesan cheese
½ tsp fresh grated nutmeg

Heat the milk and butter until it comes to the boil. Add the salt and semolina and stir until it boils — the mixture will suddenly turn very thick. Remove from the heat and quickly beat in the eggs, spinach, cheeses and nutmeg. Spoon the mixture into a well-greased shallow casserole dish (about 28 cm). Bake at 200°C for 25–35 minutes until the top is golden and crispy. Serves 5–6.

Variation: corn, pepper and chilli bake: use 2 cups whole kernel corn, 1 diced red pepper and 1 tbsp chilli sauce in place of the spinach.

Anne's Spinach Tart

My mother makes the best savoury tart I have ever tasted. It's quite quiche-like but has a denser texture and wonderful green colour. Double the recipe and freeze one — they freeze beautifully.

Preparation Time: 20 minutes
Cooking Time: 30 minutes

Pastry

1 cup plain flour
¼ tsp salt
75g butter (or ½ butter ½ lard)
about 2 tbsp cold water

Filling

⅓ cup cream cheese
3 eggs
½ cup cream or milk
1 tbsp herb pesto or 1 tbsp chopped fresh oregano
1 spring onion, chopped
1 tsp horseradish sauce
½ tsp prepared mustard
½ cup grated cheese
leaves from 2–3 heads fresh spinach (use as much or little as you prefer)
salt and pepper
pinch nutmeg

Place the flour, salt and butter in the bowl of a blender and blend to fine crumbs. With the motor running, add the water until the mixture comes together in a ball. Press into a loose-bottomed quiche dish (about 20cm), cover with baking paper and baking beans and bake blind for about 12–15 minutes at 200°C. While pastry cooks, prepare the filling. Blend together the cream cheese, eggs and cream. Add all other ingredients, blending until the mixture forms a smooth, green puree. Pour into semi-cooked pastry shell and bake at 180°C for about 30 minutes until golden. Serves 4.

Variation: Alsace Onion Tart

Fill the tart shell with a mixture made with ⅓ cup cream cheese, blended with 3 eggs and ½ cup cream or milk. Cook 4 large thinly sliced onions in 3 tbsp butter until soft but not brown. Add to the cream cheese mixture with 1 tbsp finely chopped fresh thyme, 2 tsp crushed garlic and 100g grated tasty cheese. Season to taste and bake as above.

Zucchini and Cheese Tart with Poppyseed Pastry

This light, fresh open tart is cooked directly on the baking tray. For maximum flavour, make it when zucchini is in peak supply.

Preparation Time: 15 minutes
Cooking Time: 40 minutes

Pastry

1 recipe shortcrust pastry (see spinach tart)
2 tbsp poppy seeds
1 tsp dried thyme

Zucchini and Cheese Tart with Poppyseed Pastry

Open Filo Spinach and Feta Pie

Topping

2 tbsp butter
2 onions, finely sliced
1 tsp crushed garlic
2 cups grated zucchini
salt and pepper to season
2 tbsp herb pesto
1 cup grated mozzarella cheese (or gruyere)
3 tbsp grated parmesan cheese

Mix the poppy seeds and thyme into the pastry dough. Pat out to a 25cm circle on a baking tray lined with baking paper. Prick all over with a fork. Bake at 200°C for 20 minutes until lightly golden brown. While the pastry cooks, prepare the topping. Heat the butter in a frypan and cook the onion until beginning to brown. Add the garlic and zucchini and cook until semi-dry. Season well, remove from the heat and mix in the pesto and grated cheeses. Spread over the par-cooked pastry base and bake a further 12–15 minutes at 200°C. Serves 4–5.

Open Filo, Spinach and Feta Pie

An open pie makes great use of crumbly or flakey filo that is no longer good for folding and rolling. Use your favourite quiche filling or try this great spinach and feta combination.

Preparation Time: 10 minutes
Cooking Time: 50 minutes

6 sheets filo pastry
about 50g butter, melted
1 tbsp oil
480g pack frozen spinach, thawed and drained
1 tsp crushed garlic
100g feta cheese, crumbled
3 eggs, lightly beaten
600ml milk
1 tbsp cornflour
salt, pepper and a pinch of nutmeg

Brush a sheet of filo pastry with the melted butter. Place in a 25cm flan dish. Place a sheet on top, overlapping the edges. Brush that and continue brushing and layering until you have a stack of 6 sheets. Heat the oil in a frypan and cook the spinach until it is dry. Add the garlic and cook a further minute. Spread the spinach over the base and top with crumbled feta. Mix together the eggs, milk, cornflour and seasonings. Pour over the spinach. Bake for 10 minutes at 200°C, then for 40 minutes at 160°C. Serves 6.

Protein Complements

If you are eating a purely vegetarian diet, take care to ensure you have an adequate intake of protein, vitamins and minerals.

To obtain a complete protein, consume the following foods within 2 hours of each other.

Legumes: eat with grains, cereals or nuts and seeds, eg rice or noodles with beans.

Grains and cereals: eat with legumes or with nuts and seed.

Nuts and seeds: eat with legumes, or grains and cereals.

By combining any plant foods with dairy products, you also create a complete protein.

Vegetable Platter with Green Goddess Dressing

A platter of lightly cooked vegetables served with a rich garlicky dressing makes a wonderful presentation for a first course or as part of a buffet. It's a good dish to serve in the summer when a variety of fresh vegetables are available. Vary the vegetables according to preference and availability, allowing a total of about 4–6 different vegetables per serve.

Baby potatoes and kumara (cut in chunks) — boil until just tender

Beans, beetroot, carrots and angle sliced zucchini — blanch in boiling water for 2 minutes then refresh in cold water

Pepper — roast until skins blister, then peel, deseed under running water and slice into strips

Radishes, cherry tomatoes — serve raw

Green Goddess Dressing

Preparation Time: 5 minutes

1 bunch parsley, stems removed
2 egg yolks
1–2 tsp garlic, crushed
1 tsp prepared mustard
salt and pepper
2 tsp lemon juice
about 1 cup virgin olive oil

Prepare all the vegetables and arrange on a large platter. To make the sauce, blend the parsley until finely chopped. Add the egg yolks, garlic, mustard, salt and

pepper and lemon juice. With the motor running, slowly drizzle in the oil until the sauce thickens. Makes 1½ cups. Dressing will keep for about 1 week in the fridge.

Potato Feta and Olive Slice

Mashed potatoes combine with goat's cheese and olives in a tasty breadcrumb crust in this Greek-inspired recipe. It slices well and makes a great lunch or supper dish accompanied with a simple green salad.

Preparation Time: 10 minutes
Cooking Time: 10 minutes

4 large potatoes
2 tbsp olive oil
1 tsp minced fresh thyme leaves
2 eggs
salt and pepper
2 cups fresh breadcrumbs
about 2 tbsp olive oil
125 g chevre salad cheese or feta thinly sliced
12 black olives, pitted and halved

Peel the potatoes and boil in lightly salted water until tender. Drain and dry over a very low heat. Mash to break up finely, then mash in the olive oil, thyme, eggs and salt and pepper to taste. Generously oil a straight-sided 23–25cm baking or gratin dish. Shake over two-thirds of the breadcrumbs to coat the base and sides of the dish. Spread half the mashed potato into the bread crumbed dish. Top with a layer of sliced cheese then the rest of the potatoes. Arrange the olives in a pattern over the top and sprinkle over the rest of the breadcrumbs. Bake at 200°C for 30 minutes until golden. Serve in slices. Serves 4–6.

Filo Vegetable Samoosa Parcels

Traditionally samoosas are deep-fried but baking them in filo pastry makes a lighter alternative.

Preparation Time: 20 minutes,
includes cooking of root vegetables
Cooking Time: 35–40 minutes

1 tbsp oil
1 large onion, finely diced
2 tsp each of garam masala, ground cumin and mild curry powder
1 tsp each of crushed garlic and tomato paste
3 medium potatoes, diced in 1cm pieces or 2 potatoes and a 150g wedge of pumpkin

Filo Vegetable Samoosa Parcels

Pumpkin Stuffed with Tofu and Asian Flavourings

1 medium carrot, diced as potato
1 ½ cups of water, to cook
1 cup peas, blanched
1 tsp mustard seeds
1 tsp fennel seeds, lightly crushed
salt and freshly ground pepper
20 sheets of filo
50–70g butter or margarine, melted

Heat the oil in a large heavy pan and cook the onion and spices until soft. Add the garlic and tomato paste and sizzle for a few seconds. Add the potato cubes, carrot and water. Simmer until just tender and the pan is dry. Remove from the heat, mix in the peas and season to taste. Allow the mixture to cool. Brush 1 sheet of filo with melted butter and place another on top. Butter and repeat the layers to form a stack of 5 buttered sheets. Cut the stack in half and place about 2 tbsp of filling mixture into the centre of each piece. Bring up the sides of the filo and gather to form a pouch, squeezing at the top. Place the parcels on a baking tray, then repeat the procedure with 5 more sheets to make another 2 parcels. Repeat for remaining parcels. Brush the tops of the prepared parcels with butter (they can be refrigerated for up to 24 hours at this point). Bake at 190°C for 15 minutes until golden. Serve with a crisp green salad. This recipe can be halved or doubled. Serves 8.

Pumpkin Stuffed with Tofu and Asian Flavourings

Pumpkin cooks extremely well in the microwave. This easy tofu stuffing seasoned with Asian spices makes a wonderful partner to the sweet nutty flavour of pumpkin.

Preparation Time: 15 minutes
Cooking Time: 15–18 minutes

1 medium pumpkin (800g–1kg)
2 tsp crushed garlic
1 tbsp crushed root ginger
1 tbsp sesame oil
½ cup soy sauce
250g tofu, diced in 1cm cubes
½ cup toasted sesame seeds
optional: 1 red pepper, finely sliced
1 large carrot, finely chopped
2 spring onions, chopped

Remove a lid from the pumpkin and scoop out the seeds and pith. Place the garlic and ginger in a microwave container with the sesame oil and cover on 100% power for 1 minute. Mix in the soy sauce , tofu, sesame seeds and chopped vegetables. Pile into the pumpkin cavity, replace the lid and place in a deepsided microwave dish. Add 2 tablespoons of water to the dish. Cover tightly and microwave on 100% power for 15–18 minutes — until the skin of the pumpkin gives lightly when pressed. Serves 2–3 as a main course. Alternatively, to cook conventionally, bake at 180°C for about 45 minutes, or until the pumpkin is tender.

Perfect Rice

Bring 1 cup of rice, 1¾ cups of cold water and 1 tsp of salt to the boil uncovered. Cover tightly, reduce heat and simmer 15 minutes. Turn off the heat. Do not remove lid. Leave for 15 minutes, then fluff with a fork and serve.

109

Avial (Mixed Vegetable Curry)

This dry, richly flavoured curry comes from Southern India. It can be made with any seasonal vegetables as available.

Preparation Time: 15 minutes
Cooking Time: 20 minutes

1 tbsp oil
2 tsp garam masala (available from supermarkets)
5 green chillies, chopped
1 cup desiccated coconut
½ tsp cumin seeds
1 potato, peeled and cooked
1 green banana
5 beans, 1 carrot, 2 eggplant, 1 zucchini all cut into 1.5cm dice
pinch of salt and turmeric
2 tsp oil
1 tbsp curry leaves, chopped (available from supermarkets)
½ tsp mustard seeds
½ cup natural unsweetened yoghurt
Garnish: chopped coriander leaves

Heat the oil in a large heavy-based saucepan and fry the garam masala for a few seconds. Add the chillies, coconut and cumin seeds. Stir over a low heat for 1–2 minutes. Set aside. Cut the potato in 1.5cm cubes. Place the banana (in its skin) in boiling water. Cook for about 5 minutes, until the banana is soft. Peel, discard skin and cut into 1.8cm pieces. Steam the remaining vegetables for about 5 minutes or until tender. Add the steamed vegetables to the prepared masala paste with the salt and turmeric. Toss over a low heat for 5 minutes. Add the potato and banana. Mix well. Remove from the heat. Heat the second quantity of oil in a small heavy-based pan. Stir-fry the curry leaves and mustard seeds over a low heat for 3–4 minutes. Add this to the vegetable mixture with the yoghurt. Stir to combine. Garnish with the coriander. Serve on a bed of rice. Serves 4.

Potato and Pea Curry

Poppadoms, rice, Indian pickles and yoghurt mixed with cucumber and mint turn this simple curry into a substantial vegetarian meal.

Preparation Time: 5 minutes
Cooking Time: 25 minutes

1kg potatoes
3 tbsp vegetable oil
1 tsp each of black mustard seeds and fennel seeds

1 tbsp cumin seeds
2 onions, thinly sliced
½ tsp chilli powder and black pepper and turmeric
2 tsp garam masala
2 cups peas (fresh or frozen), blanched
juice of ½ a lemon
2 tbsp chopped coriander

Wash the potatoes and boil until just tender. Drain thoroughly and cool. Meanwhile, heat the oil in a saucepan and fry the mustard, fennel and cumin seeds until they start to pop. Add the onions and remaining spices and cook until the onion softens (about 10 minutes). Cut the potatoes into wedges about 1cm thick. Add to the pan and cook over high heat until they start to brown. Mix in the peas, lemon juice and coriander and serve at once. Serves 4.

Spicy Mexican Chickpeas

The combination of nuts and legumes in this spicy one-pan dinner provides a complete protein. Serve as a main course with pita bread and sour cream or as part of a buffet with grilled meats and salads. If you don't want to make the spice mix, use a commercial Cajun Spice Mix.

Preparation Time: 10 minutes
Cooking Time: 10 minutes

2 tbsp cooking oil
2 tsp crushed garlic
2 tbsp fajita spice mix (see page 9 for recipe)
2 cans chickpeas, drained, or 3 cups cooked chickpeas
2 carrots, cut in matchsticks
½ red pepper, cut in thin strips
½ cup chopped toasted cashews
2 tbsp chopped coriander
salt and pepper

Heat the oil in a large pan and cook the garlic and spice mix for 30 seconds. Add all other ingredients, except coriander and salt and pepper, and cook over medium heat for 10 minutes, stirring frequently. Season to taste with salt and pepper and mix in the coriander. Serves 4.

Spicy Tofu and Vegetable Toss

Tofu takes on a new dimension with Asian spices. Here, flavoured with ginger, garlic, soy sauce and chilli, it makes a wonderful stir-fry meal-in-one.

Preparation Time: 5 minutes
Cooking Time: 10 minutes

Microwave Vegetarian Moussaka

1 tbsp sesame oil
2 tsp each of crushed garlic, and fresh ginger, finely chopped
250g firm tofu, diced in 2cm squares
2 tbsp soy sauce
1–2 tbsp chilli sauce
400g broccoli florets, blanched
1 pkt beansprouts
1 pkt crispy noodles
⅓ cup toasted peanuts

Heat the sesame oil in a wok or large frypan. Add the garlic and ginger and sizzle for 30 seconds. Add the tofu and cook for 1 minute. Add the soy sauce, chilli sauce and broccoli and stir to combine. Add the beansprouts, peanuts and crispy noodles and serve immediately. Serves 2–3.

Variation: In place of crispy noodles serve with rice or chinese noodles.

Microwave Vegetarian Moussaka

Microwaving makes fast work of mystic moussaka. To cook conventionally, allow about 1 hour at 180°C.

Preparation Time: 20 minutes
Cooking Time: 15–17 minutes

2×410g tins red kidney beans, drained
1 tsp crushed garlic
2 tomatoes, diced
1 tbsp chilli sauce
1 tsp dried oregano
1 eggplant, sliced thinly

400g tin tomatoes in juice, drained
¼ tsp ground nutmeg
½ tsp ground cinnamon
2 tbsp dry breadcrumbs
salt and pepper
2 tbsp butter or margarine
2½ tbsp flour
1½ cups milk
2 egg yolks
2 tsp grated parmesan cheese

Mash the beans with the garlic, tomatoes, chilli sauce and oregano. Sprinkle the eggplant with ½ tsp salt, place in a microwave bowl, cover and cook on 100% power for 5 minutes. Drain well. Cover the bottom of a micro-wave oven serving dish with half the eggplant. Put the bean mixture over this, then top with the rest of the eggplant. Puree the drained tomatoes with nutmeg, cinnamon and breadcrumbs. Season and pour over. Place the butter and flour in a microwave bowl. Cook for 1 minute on 100% power. Add the milk and mix well. Cook on 100% power for 4 minutes, stirring after 2 minutes. Beat in the egg yolks and pour over the tomato mixture. Sprinkle with the parmesan cheese, cover and cook on 50% power for 10–12 minutes or until set. Place under a preheated grill and grill for 5 minutes or until golden brown. Serves 4–5.

Vegetable Accompaniments

Quick Potato Gratin

Preparation Time: 10 minutes
Cooking Time: 30–35 minutes

8 largish potatoes (about 1kg)
80g butter
1 tsp garlic, crushed
salt and pepper

Scrub the potatoes and slice as thinly as possible. Melt the butter and mix in the garlic. Brush this all over the base and sides of a shallow medium gratin or baking dish. Layer a quarter of the potatoes evenly into the dish, brush well with butter and season with salt and pepper. Repeat the layers of potatoes, butter and seasonings. Brush the top with butter, cover the dish and microwave for 15 minutes. Leave to stand until ready to finish cooking. Leaving the potatoes in the dish, use a sharp knife to cut into 6 servings or cut out with a biscuit cutter and place on a baking tray (this is much easier than trying to cut dish neatly once it has browned). Preheat oven to 220°C and bake for 12–15 minutes until golden. Serves 6.

Crispy Kumara Cakes

Preparation Time: 10 minutes
Cooking Time: 10 minutes

1 very large or 2 small kumara, scrubbed
1 egg
1 tbsp flour
1 tsp salt
optional: 1 tsp crushed garlic or ginger
oil to cook

Grate or shred the kumara and combine with the other ingredients. Heat a little oil in a pan and cook handfuls of the mixture flattening slightly with a fish slice. Cook over medium heat until brown on both sides, (about 5 minutes on each side). Makes 6 large crisp cakes.

Flash-Roasted Potatoes with Peppers and Onions

Preparation Time: 10 minutes
Cooking Time: 15–20 minutes

4 large potatoes, washed and cut into 3–4cm pieces
2 tbsp olive oil
½ red pepper, cut into thin strips
1 small onion, thinly sliced
1 tsp crushed garlic
1 tsp chopped fresh rosemary
salt and freshly ground black pepper

Cook the potatoes in boiling water for 5 minutes. Drain thoroughly and mix with all other ingredients in a large roasting dish. Roast at 220°C for 15–20 minutes until crisp and golden, or pan fry mixture until golden. Serves 4.

Virtually all vegetables and fruits are nutritionally dense, but in the vitamin stakes certain fruits and vegetables really come up trumps. Vitamins C, D and betacarotene plus the mineral selenium (good sources are seafoods and Australian wheat) are the bodies best defence against free-radicals which are known to cause cell damage. Lettuce, cucumber, eggplant, onions and zucchini are nutrition lightweights on the A, C and E front compared to spinach, sprouts, pumpkn and broccoli.

High in vitamin C, E and betacarotene

Broccoli • tomatoes • red and green peppers • spinach • watercress • brussel sprouts • kumara • kale

High in Vitamin E

Wheatgerm oil • safflower oil • sunflower oil • sunflower seeds • almonds • avocadoes • olives

High in Vitamin C

Strawberries • oranges • kiwifruit • blackcurrants

High for Betacarotene

Carrots • rockmelons • apricots • pumpkin

Antagonists for Vitamin E

Freezing of foods • rancid foods • refined oils • estrogen • mineral oil • air pollution • chlorine • ferric forms of iron

Antagonists for Vitamin C

Exposure to oxygen • antibiotics • aspirin • cortisone • high fever • alcohol • stress • tobacco

Antagonists for Betacarotene

Alcohol • coffee • cortisone • excess iron • mineral oil • Vitamin D deficiency

Watercress and Mushroom Salad

Blanch 200g button mushrooms, drain and refresh under cold running water. Combine with 2 tbsp olive oil, 1 tbsp red wine vinegar. Leave to marinate, if desired for up to 8 hours. When ready to serve, toss with a bunch of watercress leaves and freshly ground black pepper.

Variation: add wedges of orange or diced avocado.

Chilli Sesame and Coriander Noodles

Preparation Time: 5 minutes
Cooking Time: 10–15 minutes

200g egg noodles
2 tbsp sesame oil
1 tsp chilli sauce (to taste)
2 tbsp toasted sesame seeds
¼ cup chopped fresh coriander
1 tbsp lemon juice
salt and pepper

Cook the noodles according to manufacturer's instructions. Drain and toss with all other ingredients. Serves 4 as an accompaniment.

Stir fried Vegetable Medley

Preparation Time: 10 minutes
Cooking Time: 5 minutes

I often serve this bright vegetable medley with casseroles or one-dish platters. The vegetables are blanched in advance, so all it needs is a quick toss over the heat to finish.

300g green beans
300g carrots, peeled and cut in thin strips
300g zucchinis, sliced diagonally
1 red pepper, cut in thin strips
1 tbsp olive oil or butter
2 tbsp water
1 tbsp pesto

Blanch the beans, carrots and zucchini in a large pot of boiling water for 2 minutes. Drain and refresh in cold water to prevent further cooking. Chill until required. To serve, heat the oil or butter and water in a wok or large pan and cook the vegetables, covered, for 2–3 minutes until heated through. Stir in the pesto and serve immediately.

Chinese Stir-fried Greens

Preparation Time: 5 minutes
Cooking Time: 5 minutes

600–800g prepared Chinese greens, eg bok choy, choy sum, gaai lan
1–2 tbsp oil, eg soya or peanut
¼ tsp crushed garlic
1 tsp sugar
salt to taste
optional: oyster sauce

Wash the greens and slice at an angle into segments of about 2cm, keeping the stems and leaves separate. Heat the oil in a wok or large frypan. Add the stems and toss around for a couple of minutes. Add the garlic, sugar and leaf tops and toss over the heat until the vegetables are just crisp tender (about 2–3 minutes). If necessary add a couple of tablespoons of water. Mix through a little oyster sauce and serve immediately. Serves 4.

Fresh Banana Salad

This delicious salad makes a great accompaniment to curries of all kinds. It needs to be made at the last minute or the bananas will brown.

Preparation Time: 10 minutes

2 firm bananas, peeled and sliced diagonally
½ cup natural unsweetened yoghurt
½ tsp crushed garlic
½ cup toasted coconut threads
2 tbsp chopped mint or coriander
1 tbsp lime or lemon juice
pinch each salt and pepper

Toss all ingredients to combine. Makes enough for 4–6 servings. Serve within 1 hour of making.

Greek Salad

Remove the pith and seeds from two peppers (preferably a combination of red and green). Cut the peppers and 4 fresh, firm tomatoes into 2cm chunks. Cut one small telegraph cucumber into small cubes. Dice 1 small red onion or 2 spring onions. Combine all the chopped vegetables with a dressing made from the following: ½ a cup of garlic vinaigrette dressing (see page 39), 2 tbsp each of fresh chopped mint and fresh oregano (or 2 tsp dried). Serves 4.

Desserts

Regardless of the occasion, every meal has a beginning, a middle and an end. Great desserts don't need to be relegated to special occasions or deliver a week's worth of calories in one single serve. If you are planning to finish your meal with something as simple as a piece of fresh fruit, then give it its due. Choose a delicious fruit in prime condition, and serve it on a plate with a knife. Alternatively take a few minutes extra and slice it, drizzle over a little honey and some passionfruit pulp.

Luscious cream-laden desserts work best if your menu has been light, with no cream or heavy butter sauces in any of the previous courses.

If you plan to serve cheese, it's best to do so before any sweet desserts. Your palate is still in savoury mode and the cheese provides a good link to sweet dessert tastes. Choose one or two delicious cheeses and accompany with plain cracker biscuits and fresh and dried fruits.

The Art of Delicious Fruit Salad

You don't need a lot of different fruits to make a beautiful fruit salad, even one or two will do. Choose good quality fruits and prepare them about 1 hour before serving, adding a little honey, jam or liqueur to provide a marinade that allows the fruit to form its own juices.

- Choose a range of 2–5 different fresh fruits, selecting for quality and freshness.
- Peel and slice attractively into pieces of 3–4cm (not too small).
- Spoon over about 1 tsp runny honey per serve (or liqueur, etc) and mix through.
- Add passionfruit pulp if available or a little fresh orange juice.
- Leave to stand for about 1 hour before serving.
- Add fruits that brown easily, such as bananas and pears, just before serving.

Mint and Ginger Melon Salad

When melons are plentiful this pretty salad makes a wonderfully refreshing dessert. The recipe can easily be halved or you can leave out one of the melons.

Preparation Time: 10 minutes plus standing

1 rock melon
1 honeydew melon
½ small watermelon

Syrup

¼ cup honey
¼ cup hot water
3 tbsp lemon juice
¼ cup finely chopped fresh mint
optional: 1 tbsp crushed or grated fresh root ginger

Remove the seeds and pith from the melons and either cut into small segments or use a melon baller to make melon balls. Place the prepared melon in a serving bowl and chill. Dissolve the honey in the hot water, and add the lemon juice, mint and optional ginger. Pour the syrup over the melon balls and refrigerate until ready to serve. Serves 8–10.

Variation: Berry and Melon Salad, add 1 punnet of strawberries in with the melon.

Tangelos in Caramel Syrup

This classic combination makes a refreshing dessert after a casserole or roast.

Preparation Time: 5 minutes
Cooking Time: 10 minutes

6 large tangelos
1 cup sugar
2 cups water
optional: juice of ½ lemon

Using a sharp knife, peel the tangelos carefully, leaving no pith. Slice thinly. Put the sugar in a large dry pan and melt over low heat stirring with a wooden spoon until it forms a darkish caramel. Take care not to burn. Add the water carefully, then let the mixture simmer until the caramel dissolves and a syrup is formed. Add the lemon juice. Pour over the tangelo slices and leave to cool. Serve chilled with whipped cream that can be flavoured with your favourite orange liqueur. Serves 4.

Pear and Ginger Mille-Feuille

I always try to keep a packet of brandy baskets or slices on hand for impromptu desserts. Brandy snaps are a saviour for creating smart desserts in a hurry. Fill the brandy baskets with flavoured creams and top with berries, pipe with cream mixed with nuts and chunks of chocolate and use the slices for glamorous layered concoctions like these.

Preparation Time: 10 minutes
Cooking Time: 6 minutes

8 stewed or canned pear halves, drained (or 10–12 stewed feijoas)
60g crystallised ginger
300ml cream
1 tbsp lemon juice
2 tbsp passionfruit pulp
1 tsp vanilla essence
18 round brandy slices
icing sugar

Puree the pears. Dice half of the ginger, and cut the rest into thin strips for garnishing. Whip the cream and fold into the pear puree with the diced ginger, lemon juice, passionfruit pulp and vanilla. Top 1 biscuit with 2 tbsp fruit cream. Place a biscuit on top. Cover with another 2 tbsp fruit cream and top with a final biscuit. Continue for the remaining biscuits. Sprinkle with a little icing sugar and garnish with strips of ginger. Serves 6.

Warm Harvest Fruit Salad with Meringue Gratin

This yummy meringue makes a stylish finish to fresh fruit salad. If preferred, the meringue can be cooked in advance and served over room temperature fruit.

Preparation Time: 15 minutes
Cooking time: 1–2 minutes

1.3kg mixed seasonal fresh fruit of at least 4 kinds, eg kiwifruit, grapes, pears, apples, feijoas, bananas, cape gooseberries
2 tbsp dark runny honey
½ cup passionfruit pulp
2 egg whites
½ cup sugar
1 tsp vanilla essence
½ cup toasted coconut
optional: 2 tbsp brandy, ¼ cup finely chopped walnuts

Warm Harvest Fruit Salad with Meringue Gratin

Slice the fruit and macerate for at least 1 hour with the honey and passionfruit pulp, leaving out the bananas and other fruit that may discolour. Use an electric beater to beat the egg whites and sugar until they form a shiny, smooth meringue (about 10 minutes). Mix in the vanilla, toasted coconut and walnuts. Just before serving, spoon the fruit onto 6 ovenproof serving plates and top with a spoonful of meringue. Flatten the meringue lightly and swirl the tops. Place plates under a preheated grill for 1–2 minutes until lightly browned. If desired, flambe with a little heated brandy or Drambuie. Serves 6.

Fabulous Fruit Salad

I try and serve fresh fruit in some form or other most evenings as dessert - it's palate cleaning and refreshing as well as being very nutritious. If you want to glamorise a fresh fruit dessert bring in a flavoured cream or some ice cream or sorbet, shavings of white chocolate or a little sweet biscuit. Or you could pile the fruit into a cooked pastry case, atop a layer of custard or vanilla dairy food.

Combinations

• Strawberries, icing sugar and Drambuie
• Kiwifruit, pears, honey and passionfruit
• Pureed strawberries and icing sugar mixed through watermelon wedges
• Sliced oranges with Grand Marnier
• Fresh pineapple wedges, sliced kiwifruit, pawpaw wedges, sliced bananas and if desired, fresh sliced feijoas or pears
• Pureed strawberries with mango slices
• Melon, honey and fresh ginger

Parfait Perfect

Whipped cream or yoghurt, layered or folded with fresh or dried fruits, nuts, crumbled biscuits or chocolate makes a heavenly dessert that's easy to assemble. Every year there seems to be a new combination that does the rounds, but the old favourite of whipped cream, folded with boysenberries, chopped marshmallows and chunks of white chocolate is always popular. Next time you feel like a parfait-styled dessert try one of these easy combinations — many of them use yoghurt which is a lot lighter on the palate.

Boysenberry Ginger Parfait

Mix 2 cups fresh or frozen boysenberries (or other berries) with 2 cups fruit yoghurt or 1 cup cream, whipped and 3 crumbled brandy snaps. Sweeten if desired with 2 tbsp runny honey. Serve chilled.

Amaretto Apricot Ginger Parfait

Gingernut logs bring to mind the 70s. Resurrect them for the 90s with delicious liqueurs, fruit purees and nuts.

Preparation Time: 10 minutes

300ml cream
100g dark chocolate, diced
50g glace ginger, chopped
4 cooked apricot halves, pureed
1 pkt gingernuts, broken into bits
about ½ cup Amaretto
garnish: toasted chopped hazelnuts, dried apricots
  and ginger

Whip the cream and fold in the chocolate, ginger and apricot. Dunk the gingernuts in amaretto and fold into the cream. Pile into tall glasses and garnish with apricot, ginger and hazelnuts. Serves 4–6.

Elizabeth David's Cremets d'Angers

This is a yummy spoonable cream that can be served with fruit salad, pears in red wine, dried fruit compotes or any dessert cake.

For every 300ml of cream, allow 2 egg whites

Whip the cream until stiff, then whip the whites in another bowl until they form stiff peaks. Carefully fold the whites into the cream. Pour into a muslin-lined sieve and leave to drain in a cool place overnight or for at least 3 hours. Serve turned out with liquid cream poured over the top.

Strawberry Fool

Delicious fruit fools are simple to prepare. Choose fruit that purees well and has a good acidity, such as plums or apricots, strawberries, gooseberries or other berry fruit.

Preparation Time: 10 minutes

1 punnet strawberries, hulled
2 tbsp icing sugar
1 tbsp lemon juice
300ml cream, whipped

Blend the strawberries to a puree with the icing sugar and lemon juice. Fold into the whipped cream. Serves 4.

Tiramisu

The trendiest dessert of the 90s, tiramisu is usually made with marscapone cheese, which makes it heavy and rich. I prefer my Italian trifle made with whipped cream, but be warned, this version is dreadfully moreish. It benefits from being made a day in advance.

Preparation Time: 10 minutes plus chilling

2 cups cream
1 tbsp icing sugar
1 tsp vanilla essence
100g dark chocolate, chopped
2 tbsp sugar
1 large cup very strong black coffee
¼ cup brandy or cognac
1 chocolate sponge, cut in half horizontally, then
  sliced into 4cm-thick strips

Whip the cream to soft peaks with the icing sugar and the vanilla. Fold in the chocolate. Dissolve the sugar in the coffee and mix in the brandy. Have a shallow serving dish ready, quickly pass the sponge fingers one at a time through the coffee mix (don't let them sit in there) and lay in a single layer in the base of a large shallow serving dish. Spoon over a third of the cream mixture. Dunk remaining sponge pieces in the coffee mix one at a time, forming another layer on top of the cream mixture. Repeat until the sponge is all used. Top with the rest of the cream mix, spreading it evenly. Sprinkle with sifted cocoa or coffee powder. Refrigerate for at least 1 hour (or up to 12 hours) before serving. Serves 6.

Apricot Zabaglione

Light as air, with an intense taste of apricots, zabaglione is a dessert you have to make at the last moment.

Preparation Time: 10 minutes
Cooking Time: 3–4 minutes

100g dried apricots (other fruits may be used)
1 cup water
250g sugar
12 egg yolks
½ cup Marsala

Soak the apricots in the water until plump. Place in a saucepan with the sugar. Bring to the boil and simmer until the apricots are soft. Remove them from the syrup (reserving) and chop into small pieces or roughly puree. Place the egg yolks, Marsala and ½ cup of the apricot syrup in a copper or metal bowl and whisk until the mixture becomes light and foamy. Place the bowl over a double boiler and whisk constantly and vigorously until the zabaglione is quite stiff. (If you are brave you can do it directly over the heat.) Fold in the apricots, mix well and serve immediately in tall glasses. Serves 6.

Chantilly Ice with Fresh Berry Coulis

Flavoured whipped cream, folded with beaten egg whites and crumbled meringue, then frozen, makes a wonderfully impressive dessert that cuts well and eats like a dream. Once made, the chantilly ice can be stored tightly covered in the freezer for 2–3 weeks.

Preparation Time: 10 minutes plus freezing

3 egg whites
pinch of salt
⅓ cup sugar
400ml cream
1 tsp vanilla essence
8 meringues
optional: 2 tbsp of liqueur of your choice

Berry Coulis

2 cups raspberries or blackberries
2 tbsp icing sugar

Pear and Ginger Mille-feuille; Tiramisu

Whip the egg whites with the salt until they form peaks. Slowly add the sugar and beat until very stiff. Whip the cream with the vanilla until it holds its shape. Crumble the meringues and fold into the cream with the egg whites. Place in a 20–22cm tin with a removable bottom lined with plastic wrap, or a shallow dish also lined. Cover and freeze for 3–4 hours or until firm. Unmould onto a serving plate and slice to serve. Serve with a fresh berry coulis. To prepare coulis, puree berries with icing sugar, then strain into a jug. Serves 6–8.

Old-Fashioned Favourites

Everyone loves substantial old-fashioned desserts like crumbles, rice puddings and apple pie — they're the comfort food of the 90s.

Spiced Apple and Berry Crumble

Really fast fruit crumbles can be made using a tin of apples and a muesli topping. This one takes a little more time but provides a great traditional flavour.

Preparation Time: 25 minutes
Cooking Time: 30 minutes

1 cup flour
1 cup brown sugar
1 cup rolled oats
1 tbsp cinnamon
2 tsp ground ginger
1 tsp nutmeg
½ cup (125g) butter
optional: 50g walnuts, chopped
5–6 apples (1kg), peeled, cored and sliced
2 cups berry fruit, drained of any liquid, eg raspberries, blackberries, blueberries

Combine the flour, sugar, oats and spices in a bowl. Gently rub in the butter until the mixture resembles breadcrumbs. Add the walnuts. Combine the apples and berry fruit in a microwave bowl, cover and cook on 100% power for 5 minutes (or stew until soft). Place the fruit with its juice in the bottom of a 26–28cm pie-dish. Sprinkle the crumble mixture over the top. Bake at 180°C for 30 minutes until topping is crisp. Serves 6.

Fresh Peaches with Ginger Crumble

This easy crumble topping is delicious atop fresh peaches. It would also be nice with apricots or as a topping for cooked apples.

Preparation Time: 5 minutes
Cooking Time: 20 minutes

6 fresh peaches, halved and stones removed
4 crushed gingernuts (or 8 crushed amaretti biscuits)
1 tbsp brown sugar
50g butter

Place the peach halves, cutside up in a baking dish. Combine the gingernuts, sugar and butter and divide over the top of the peaches. Bake at 180°C for about 20 minutes until the peaches are semi-soft. Serves 6.

Creamy Rice Pudding

Short grain rice is the key to creamy rice pudding. Stirring the rice as it cooks also helps to create a creamy result.

Preparation Time: 5 minutes
Cooking Time: 20 minutes

optional: ⅓ cup sultanas or raisins
4 cups milk
1 cup short grain rice
3 tbsp honey or sugar
finely grated rind of ½ a lemon
generous pinch nutmeg
1 tsp vanilla essence
optional: 2–3 tbsp cream

Place all the ingredients in a saucepan and stir over a low heat for about 20 minutes, until the mixture is creamy and the rice is cooked through. Serve hot or cold.

To microwave, mix 1½ tbsp cornflour in with the milk and place with all other ingredients in a large microwave bowl. Cover tightly and cook at 70% power for 8 minutes, stirring twice. Reduce power to 50% and cook a further 11 minutes, stirring every 3 minutes, until the rice is cooked and creamy. Serve hot or cold. Serves 4.

Tamarillo Clafoutis

Preparation Time: 10 minutes
Cooking Time: 25 minutes

Batter

½ cup flour
pinch salt
½ tsp baking powder
¼ cup sugar
3 eggs
1 cup milk
1 tsp vanilla essence

To Cook

30g butter, melted
6 peeled and sliced tamarilloes

Beat together the batter ingredients. Preheat a sponge roll tin or small roasting dish with the butter for 5 minutes at 220°C. Peel and slice the tamarilloes. Arrange in the heated dish and quickly pour over the batter. Sprinkle over 1 tbsp sugar and bake at 220°C for 12–15 minutes, until the clafoutis is puffed, golden and cooked through. To test if cooked push a skewer into the centre of the clafoutis, if it comes out clean the mixture is cooked. Serve warm or at room temperature. Serves 6. Clafoutis is also delicious made with apples — add 1 tsp cinnamon to the batter mixture.

Other variations

1 In place of tamarilloes use wedges of fresh pear and drizzle with passionfruit pulp.
2 Use any stone-fruit or berry fruit.
3 Add 1 tbsp of grated root ginger to the cake batter.

Fresh Fruit Custard Flan

Ready-made pastry and carton custard make fast work of an attractive fresh fruit flan. Top with sliced seasonal fruits as available.

Preparation Time: 15 minutes
Cooking Time: 30 minutes

400g shortcrust pastry
3 cups prepared custard (can use ready-made)
8–10 kiwifruit, peeled and sliced
1 chip strawberries, hulled and halved

Glaze

¼ cup apricot jam

Roll out the pastry to line a 24cm flan dish. Place a circle of greaseproof paper in base. Half fill with dry beans. Bake at 200°C for 15 minutes. Remove beans and paper and bake at 180°C for a further 15 minutes until golden and crisp. Cool. Spread the custard into cool pastry shell. Arrange the kiwifruit and strawberries in an overlapping pattern on top. Melt the jam and strain through a sieve. Brush over the fruit to glaze. Chill. Serves 8–10.

Variation: Instead of custard, fill the flan with a mixture of 150g cream cheese blended with 150ml vanilla dairy food.

Apple Krummeltorte

This is my favourite apple pie. It's more of a deep short-cake than a pie, but it has a wonderful flavour. Canned apple slices streamline the process.

Apple Krummeltorte; Fresh Fruit Custard Flan

Preparation Time: 15 minutes
Cooking Time: 20–25 minutes

Pastry

75g butter
100g castor sugar
1 egg
2 tsp vanilla essence
2½ cups self-raising flour

Filling

1 tin apple slices (550g) (or 2 cups cooked fruit of your choice, drained)
2 tbsp castor sugar
1 tsp cinnamon
grated rind of 1 orange

Beat the butter and sugar until fluffy, then beat in the egg and vanilla. Mix in the flour and work until the mixture forms a ball (it will be slightly dry). Press three-quarters of the pastry into the base of a 20–22cm loose-bottomed cake tin, taking it 3cm up the sides. Fill with the apple, sprinkle with castor sugar, cinnamon and grated orange rind. Crumble the remaining pastry over the top. Bake 20–25 minutes at 220°C until golden. Serve warm or cold. Serves 6–8.

Greek Orange Syrup Cake

Syrup cakes make wonderful dessert fare. They are foolproof, as the syrup virtually ensures the cakes will always be moist.

Preparation Time: 15 minutes plus chilling
Cooking Time: 40 minutes

1 cup sugar
5 eggs, separated
finely grated rind and juice of 2 oranges
225g unsalted butter, melted
1 cup flour
3½ tsp baking powder

Syrup

2 cups water
1 cup sugar
finely grated rind of 1 orange
50ml orange liqueur
finely grated rind of 1 lemon
juice of 1 lemon
garnish: whipped cream, chocolate shavings.

Preheat oven to 190°C. Cream the sugar, egg yolks and orange rind. Stir in the melted butter, orange juice, flour and baking powder. Carefully fold in the stiffly beaten egg whites. Pour into an 18 or 20cm greased, lined tin. Bake for 10 minutes, then lower temperature to 150°C and bake a further 30 minutes or until a skewer comes out clean. While the cake is baking, heat the syrup ingredients, boiling gently for 5 minutes. Cool, pour the cooled syrup over the hot cake. Chill the cake. Garnish with whipped cream and shavings of chocolate. Serves 6–8.

Dark Rich Chocolate Sauce

This shiny chocolate sauce makes a great accompaniment to chocolate cake or ice cream.

Preparation Time: 3 minutes
Cooking Time: 2 minutes

20g unsalted butter
½ cup cream
250g bittersweet chocolate

In a small saucepan heat the butter and cream until the butter melts. Chop the chocolate into small pieces. Incorporate the chocolate into warmed cream and mix until smooth. If you desire a thinner chocolate sauce, thin with warm water. Makes about 1½ cups.

Variation: use a large Moro bar in place of the chocolate.

Surprise Chocolate Cake

Vegetables, whether they be carrots, zucchinis or pumpkins add moisture to cakes and muffins without any discernible flavour.

Preparation Time: 15 minutes
Cooking Time: 50 minutes

3 eggs
1 cup brown sugar
½ cup white sugar
1 tsp vanilla essence
125g butter, softened
½ cup plain, unsweetened yoghurt
250g peeled, seeded pumpkin, grated
250g choc bits or chips
2½ cups flour
¼ cup cocoa
2 tsp baking soda
1 tsp cinnamon
½ tsp mixed spice

In a food processor or using a beater, mix together the eggs, sugars and vanilla. Add the butter and yoghurt, blending until smooth. Fold in the pumpkin and chocolate bits and combined dry ingredients. Mix gently to combine. Spread into a greased 26cm tin and bake at 180°C for about 50 minutes. Allow to cool before turning out and icing. Serves 8.

Lemon Honey and Raspberry Flan

Lemon honey makes a great tart filling that will keep in the fridge for weeks.

Preparation Time: 10 minutes
Cooking Time: 5 minutes microwave

3 large juicy lemons (juice and rind)
200g sugar
80g butter
3 eggs
1x26–28cm cooked shortcrust pastry shell
1 punnet raspberries
icing sugar to dust

In a microwave bowl or double boiler place the finely grated rind and juice of the lemons, sugar and butter. Microwave on 100% power for 3 minutes. To cook conventionally, place in a double boiler and cook until thickened. Beat 3 eggs and whisk into the mixture. Microwave on 100% power for 1 minute, beat well, then microwave for a further minute. Spread the mixture into a cooked pastry shell. Decorate with raspberries and sieve over icing sugar. Serves 6–8.

Pears in Red Wine with Oriental Spices

Pears in Red Wine with Oriental Spices

Heady spices update this classic dessert. The pears are best cooked a day ahead and left overnight for the colour to soak through.

Preparation Time: 5 minutes
Cooking Time: 20–25 minutes

4 cups red wine
2 tbsp dark honey
2 cinnamon sticks
rind of ½ orange (no pith)
2 tsp whole black peppercorns
3–4 bayleaves
2cm fresh root ginger, cut into thin matchstick strips
optional: 3 whole star anise,
         1 tbsp grenadine (for colour)
8 firm pears
½ cup Drambuie, warmed

Combine the wine and all other ingredients, except the pears and Drambuie, in a medium to large pot (to fit pears tightly in a single layer) and bring to a simmer. Peel the pears, leaving stalks intact. Place in syrup (there should be enough to at least three-quarters cover the pears). Simmer for 20–25 minutes, turning regularly (4–5 times) during cooking. Leave to cool in the syrup, turning once or twice. Remove the pears from the syrup and reserve. Reduce the syrup by half. Pour the hot syrup over the pears, spoon over the warm Drambuie and light. Serves 8.

Dried Fruit Compote

Ray McVinnie from Auckland's Metropole restaurant demonstrated this wonderful compote at one of our classes here at the Culinary Institute. His richly flavoured brew of fruits and nuts will keep for weeks in the fridge.

Preparation Time: 10 minutes plus standing
Cooking Time: 5 minutes

3 cups dried fruit, eg apricots, raisins, figs, peaches,
   pears, currants, a few cherries
½ cup blanched almonds
2 apples, cored, peeled and sliced
rind of 1 orange
1 tsp cardamom seeds, pods discarded, seeds crushed
6 whole cloves
5cm stick of cinnamon
1 cup brown sugar
juice of 1 lemon
1 cup red wine
1 cup water

Mix everything well and leave to stand for 2 hours. Pour the mixture into a saucepan, bring to the boil, simmer 5 minutes or until fruit is soft and plump. Chill. Makes about 1 litre. Serves 6–8.

Banana and Coconut Filo Parcels with Spiced Sugar

Preparation Time: 10 minutes
Cooking Time: 20 minutes

I first made these yummy little parcels as deep-fried wontons but filo pastry is much less hassle and tastes just as good.

2 large bananas, peeled — angle sliced
1 tbsp lemon juice
¼ cup toasted coconut
1 tbsp sugar
12 sheets filo pastry
about 50g melted butter
icing sugar
ground ginger
cinnamon

Combine the sliced bananas with the lemon juice, coconut and sugar. Brush a sheet of filo with the melted butter, top with another sheet then fold into quarters. Place 3–4 pieces of banana in the centre and bring up to sides to form a purse. Repeat to form 6 purses. Bake at 180°C for 20 minutes until golden. Combine the icing sugar with ginger and cinnamon and dust the parcels. Serves 6.

Freeform Filo Fruit Parcels

Brush a sheet of filo pastry with melted butter or oil. Scrunch up to form a nest shape. Spoon about 2–3 tbsp cooked, sweetened fruit into the centre, dust with sugar and bake at 190°C for 12–15 minutes until golden.

Filling combinations

- Stewed feijoas and ginger
- Cooked apples, cinnamon, cloves and pistachio nuts
- Sliced, cooked plum halves with a pinch of 5-spice powder
- Canned peach slices with coconut and mixed spice

Sweet Treats

Sometimes at the end of a meal all you feel like is a little sweet treat, such as a morsel of fudge or a dried apricot slice. Here is a selection of my favourite after-dinner treats.

Apricot Almond Fudge

Preparation Time: 10 minutes plus chilling
Cooking Time: 4 minutes

200g butter
100g brown sugar
½ tin sweetened condensed milk
500g superwine biscuits, crushed finely (2 pkts)
100g dried apricots, finely diced
finely grated rind of ½ lemon
¼ tsp almond essence

Icing

50g melted butter
300g icing sugar
1–2 tbsp boiling water to mix
1 tsp vanilla essence
dash almond essence
garnish: whole toasted almonds

Place the butter, sugar and condensed milk in a large heatproof microwave bowl and cover loosely. Microwave on 100% power for 4 minutes, stirring well every minute. Remove from the microwave and mix in all other ingredients. Press the mixture into a sponge-roll tin and chill for about 20 minutes before icing. To ice, combine the butter and icing sugar with enough water to make a spreadable icing. Mix in the vanilla and almond essences. Spread over slice and dot with whole toasted almonds. Chill until icing has set, then cut into bars.

Chocolate and Cherry Slice

Preparation Time: 10 minutes
Cooking Time: 15–20 minutes

300g dark chocolate
250g glace cherries
1 large egg
125g castor sugar
150g thread coconut

Line a swiss-roll tin with foil. Melt the chocolate and spread over the base of the tin. Mix together the remaining ingredients and spread over the chocolate. Bake at 180°C for 15–20 minutes. Cool, then chill before slicing. Makes 24 bars.

An Assortment of Chocolate Truffles

Chocolate Truffles

Preparation time: 10 minutes

200ml cream
50g unsalted butter
¼ cup liqueur of your choice
450g dark chocolate, preferably Belgian or white
  chocolate
dark or white chocolate or cocoa for dipping.

Heat the cream and butter until the butter is melted, then remove it from the heat and allow to cool slightly. Mix in the liqueur and any other flavourings of your choice, then add the broken chocolate and stir until the mixture is smooth. Refrigerate until firm enough to roll into balls. Form into small balls then chill again before dipping into either melted chocolate or rolling in cocoa or ground nuts. Makes 30–36.

Variations

Grand Marnier: Use grand marnier liqueur and dust with cocoa. Garnish with crystallised orange rind.

Creme de Menthe: Use creme de menthe liqueur and roll in toasted ground hazelnuts or top with sliced dried fruits.

Baileys Irish Cream: Use Baileys and dip into white chocolate, top with half a pistachio nut.

Supreme: Use white chocolate for the mixture add ½ cup sultanas and dip into white chocolate. Garnish with a hazelnut.

Apricot and Nut Rocky Road Slice

Preparation Time: 10 minutes
Cooking Time: 5 minutes

400g dark chocolate, broken into pieces
1 tin sweetened condensed milk
¼ cup icing sugar
2 tsp vanilla essence
150g chopped dried apricots
200g toasted hazelnuts or almonds

Place the chocolate and condensed milk in a large microwave bowl. Cook on 100% power for 4 minutes, stirring every minute. Stir until smooth. Stir in the icing sugar and vanilla. Blend in remaining ingredients and pour into a sponge-roll tin lined with waxed paper. Chill until firm, then cut into chunks. Keep in a cool place. Makes about 30 squares.

125

Index

Appetisers

Antipasto Platter	22
Base Fritter Batter	17
Basil Aioli Dip	12
Cajun Pork Balls	17
Cashew Nut Dipping Sauce	12
Cheat's Mini Pizzas	16
Cheese and Fruit Platters	22
Chicken Liver Crostini	14
Chilled Oysters with Shinto Dressing	18
Chilli Smoked Mussel Rice Cakes	21
Corn, Chilli and Coriander Fritters	17
Crispy Vegetable Rice Cakes	21
Crostini and Bruschetta Topping Combinations	15
Crostini Bread Bases	15
Fritters	17
Garlic and Lemon Squid	20
Garlic Pita Crisps	12
Herb and Feta Frittata	16
Herbed Black Olives	16
Marinated Fish or Scallops	20
Mussels on Half Shell with Wine and Herbs	20
Mussels on Half Shell with Pesto Vinaigrette	19
Poppadom Bites	12
Preparing Vegetable Crudites	12
Salmon Sates with Sesame Mayonnaise	13
Salmon Tartare	18
Seafood Platters	20
Sesame Mayonnaise	12
Smoked Fish Fritters	17
Smoked Salmon Frittata	16
Smoked Salmon Rice Cakes	21
Thai Chicken Skewers	13
Thai Curry Dipping Sauce	12
Thai Shrimp Dip	12
Tortellini and Ravioli	12
Tuna Sashimi	18
Venison Carpaccio	18
Water Chestnut and Bacon Wraps	13
Whitebait Fritters	17

Breads and Flour Based Dishes

Base Fritter Batter	17
Cheat's Mini Pizzas	16
Chicken Liver Crostini	14
Crostini and Bruschetta Topping Combinations	15
Crostini Bread Bases	15
Croutons	30
Dumplings	101
Focaccia Bread	30
Fried Croutons	30
Garlic Oil Croutons	30
Garlic Pita Crisps	12
Gourmet Burgers	98
Pesto Croutons	30
Pizza	31
Poppadom Bites	12
Shortcrust Pastry	106
Tahitian Fish Sandwich	65
Tapenade Croutons	30
Texan Corn Bread	30
Whole Baked Fish Sandwiches	65

Chicken

Cantonese Chicken and Vegetables	80
Caribbean Chicken	82
Chicken and Bean Pan-fry	76
Chicken and Broccoli with Black Bean Sauce	79
Chicken and Noodles with Chilli Peanut Sauce	77
Chicken and Spinach Curry	77
Chicken Liver Crostini	14
Chicken Skewers marinated with Yoghurt and Indian Spices	76
Chicken with Lemon and Herbs	78
Chicken, Baby Corn and Pepper Stir-fry	80
Coq Au Vin	86
Creamy Chicken and Bean Daube	83
Creamy Pasta with Bacon, Chicken, Hazelnuts and Beans	49
Duck and Mushroom Fettuccine	44
Duck Risotto	51
Fast-track Roasting	86
Harvest Chicken Pot Pie	84
Italian Pot-Roasted Chicken with Garlic and Herbs	85
Kashmir Chicken Stir-fry	80
Kentucky Baked Chicken with Creamy Corn and Thyme Sauce	82
Pasta with Country Chicken Sauce	47
Quick Homemade Chicken Stock	9
Roasting	86
Sauteed Chicken Breasts with White Wine, Mushrooms & tarragon	81
Sesame Schnitzels with fresh Banana Salsa	78
Spicy Chicken Couscous with Roasted Peppers and fresh Green Beans	84
Spicy Chicken Mole	76
Spicy Portuguese Chicken Saute	82
Tandoori Roasted Chicken	87
Thai Chicken Curry	78
Thai Chicken Skewers	13
Thai Smoked Chicken Salad	34
Warm Chicken Liver Salad	40
Warm Chicken Salad with Chilli Peanut Dressing	41

Desserts

Amaretto Apricot Ginger Parfait	118
Apple Krummeltorte	121
Apricot Zabaglione	119
Banana and Coconut Filo Parcel with Spiced Sugar	124
Boysenberry Ginger Parfait	118
Chantilly Ice with Fresh Berry Coulis	119
Creamy Rice Pudding	120
Dark Rich Chocolate Sauce	122
Dried Fruit Compote	123
Elizabeth David's Cremets d'Angers	118
Freeform Filo Fruit Parcels	124
Fresh Fruit Custard Flan	121
Fresh Peaches with Ginger Crumble	120
Greek Orange Syrup Cake	122
Lemon Honey and Raspberry Flan	122
Mint and Ginger Melon Salad	116
Pear and Ginger Mille-Feuille	116
Pears in Red Wine with Oriental Spices	123
Spiced Apple and Berry Crumble	120
Strawberry Fool	118
Surprise Chocolate Cake	122
Tamarillo Clafoutis	120
Tangelos in Caramel Syrup	116
The Art of Delicious Fruit Salad	116
Tiramisu	118
Warm Harvest Fruit Salad with Meringue Gratin	117

Dips, and Sauces and Dressings

Aioli	9
Avocado Sauce (with Pan-fried Fish)	62
Basic Vinaigrette Dressing	39
Basil Aioli	12
Basil Pesto	9
Berry Sauce for Lamb, Beef or Venison	96
Cashew Nut Dipping Sauce	12
Chilli Ratatouille	104
Chunky Guacamole Salsa	64

Corn and Pepper Salsa 65
Crayfish with Flavoured Butter 56
Curry Spice 9
Dark Rich Chocolate Sauce 122
Dark Rich Mushroom Sauce 105
Fajita Spice Mix 9
Flavoured Butters 56
Fresh Banana Salsa 65
Garlic Dressing 39
Garlic Pine Nut Butter 56
Garlic, Basil and Anchovy Dipping
    Sauce 99
Gravy 97
Greek Salad 113
Green Goddess Dressing 108
Green Peppercorn Butter 56
Green Peppercorn Sauce for
    Steaks 94
Homemade Mayonnaise 39
Kiwifruit and Pawpaw Salsa 64
Light Fume & Brie Sauce (with
    Pan-fried Salmon Steaks) 62
Mayonnaise — The Best 39
Mexican Tomato Salsa 64
On-the-spot Dressing for Greens 39
Peach and Mint Salsa 64
Pesto 9
Pesto Cream Sauce (with Cockles or
    Mussels) 61
Provencal Bean and Eggplant
    Sauce 105
Red Pepper Butter 56
Sesame Ginger Butter 56
Sesame Mayonnaise 12
Shinto Dressing for Oysters 18
Spicy Cashew Sauce (with Pan-fried
    Fish) 62
Sundried Tomato Pesto 9
Tapenade 9
Thai Shrimp Dip 12
Walnut Dressing 39
Winter Parsley Pesto 9
Yoghurt Sauce for Felafels 104

Drinks

Champagne Cocktails 23
Kiwi Coladas 22
60s Fruit Punch 22
Sludgy Margaritas 22
Trinidad Cooler 22

First Courses and Small Plates

Asparagus Salad with Cashews, Bacon
    and Oranges 38
Avocado, Bacon and Banana Salad 35
Brie, Bacon and Avocado Salad 37
Caesar Salad 34
Chicken Liver Crostini 14

Chilled Oysters with Shinto
    Dressing 18
Chilli Smoked Mussel Rice Cakes 21
Cockles or Mussels with Pesto
    Cream 61
Corn, Chilli and Coriander Fritters 17
Garlic and Lemon Squid 20
Marinated Fish or Scallops 20
Marinated Mozzarella with Baby
    Tomatoes and Pickled Walnuts 38
Mediterranean Skewered Fish and
    Vegetables 54
Miso Soup 29
Moroccan Pumpkin Soup 26
Mussels on Half Shell with Pesto
    Vinaigrette 19
Mussels on Half Shell with Wine and
    Herbs 20
Salad of Roasted Fresh Walnuts and
    Grilled Hipi-iti 34
Salmon Sates with Sesame
    Mayonnaise 13
Salmon Tartare 18
Smoked Fish Fritters 17
Smoked Salmon Rice Cakes 21
Spicy Tomato Spare Ribs 98
Straciatella Soup 29
Sushi Rice Cakes 21
Thai Chicken Skewers 13
Thai Mussels with Chilli and
    Coriander 27
Tom Yum Soup 29
Vegetable Crudites 12
Venison Carpaccio 18
Whitebait Fritters 17
Wild Mushroom Soup 27

Hints

Chilli 91
Cooking Pasta for a Party 44
Dried Mushrooms 27
Filo as a Wrapper 59
Flavour Boosters 29
Flavoured Oils 57
Free-form Filo Fruit Parcels 124
How To Butterfly A Bird 86
How to Select and Store Fish 61
Matching the Fish with the Method 60
Opening Shellfish 57
Perfect Rice 109
Saute Ideas for Chicken 81
Skewers 54
The Art of Delicious Fruit Salad 116
The Press Test for Doneness of
    Meat 96
To Blanch Spinach 83
To Prepare Fish in Parcels 70
Vegetable Purees 105
Vegetarian Nutrition 108
Whole Baked Fish Sandwiches 65
When Mayonnaise or Guacamole
    Curdles 34

Meat

90s Roast Meat and Vegetables 96
Beef Nicoise 94
Berry Sauce for Lamb, Beef or
    Venison 96
Black Bean and Chilli Beef
    Noodles 90
Braised Oxtails with Red Chilli
    Beans 100
Cajun Pork Balls 17
China Coast Beef and Noodles 92
Cooking the Perfect Steak —
    hint box 94
Dumplings 101
Ginger Pork and Broccoli 92
Gourmet Burgers 98
Honey Mustard Crust for Lamb
    Racks 96
Hungarian Pepper and Beef
    Goulash 95
Italian Rabbit with Mint and
    Pinenuts 100
Lamb and Beans with Indian
    Spices 93
Lamb Chwarma Pockets 98
Lamb Racks with Kiwifruit Chutney
    Dipping Sauce 96
Lamb Rumps with Sundried Tomatoes
    and Prunes 101
Mediterranean Summer Grill Plate 99
Mexican Lamb or Beef Fajitas 90
Oriental Pork Salad 36
Quick Roasts for Lamb Racks 96
Pan-fried Beef Steaks with Vegetable
    Chilli 91
Pan-fried Cervena Venison with
    Tapenade and Peppers 94
Pork Fillets with Tomato Honey
    Glaze 90
Rack of Lamb with Minted Zucchini
    Stuffing 96
Spicy Tomato Spare Ribs 98
Steak, Mushroom and Kidney
    Pudding 101
Steaks with Green Peppercorn
    Sauce 94
Stir-frying Technique for Meat Dishes
    — hint box 93
Texas Chilli 92
The Press Test for Doneness of
    Meat — hint box 96
To Make A Gravy — hint box 97
Venison Carpaccio 18
Venison Salad with Watercress and
    Wild Berry Dressing 41

Nutrition

Protein Complements for
    Vegetarians 108
Vitamin and Mineral Contents of
    Vegetables 112

One Dish Dining

American Mussel and Corn
  Chowder   28
Beef Nicoise   94
Black Bean and Chilli Beef
  Noodles   90
Braised Oxtails with Red Chilli
  Beans   100
Chicken and Bean Pan-fry   76
Chicken and Noodles with Chilli
  Peanut Sauce   77
Chicken and Spinach Curry   77
China Coast Beef and Noodles   92
Coq Au Vin   86
Fast-track Roast Chicken and
  Vegetables   86
French Mussel and Fennel Pan   68
Ginger Pork and Broccoli   92
Harvest Chicken Pot Pie   84
Hungarian Pepper and Beef
  Goulash   95
Italian Pot-Roasted Chicken with
  Garlic and Herbs   85
Lamb and Beans with Indian
  Spices   93
Lamb Rumps with Sundried Tomatoes
  and Prunes   101
Mango Prawns from Hell   63
Mediterranean Squid   58
Mexican Mussel Soup   28
Microwave Vegetarian Moussaka   111
Mussel Soup   28
Paella   71
Pan-fried Beef Steaks with Vegetable
  Chilli   91
Potato and Pea Curry   110
Smoked Fish and Kumara Pie   70
Smoked Ham Soup with White Beans
  and Mint   26
Spicy Chicken Couscous with Roasted
  Peppers and fresh Green Beans   84
Spicy Chicken Mole   76
Spicy Mexican Chickpeas   110
Spicy Sausage and Chickpea
  Minestrone   26
Spicy Tofu and Vegetable Toss   110
Steak, Mushroom and Kidney
  Pudding   101
Texas Chilli   92
Thai Chicken Curry   78
Thai Fish Curry   60
Thai Mussels with Chilli and
  Coriander   27
Veracruz Fish Bake   68

Pasta and Rice

Chilli Mussel Fettuccine   47
Chilli Sesame and Coriander
  Noodles   113
Creamy Pasta and Scallops   50
Creamy Pasta with Bacon, Chicken,
  Hazelnuts and Beans   49
Duck and Mushroom Fettuccine   44
Duck Risotto   51
Fettuccine with Ham Broccoli and
  Pinenuts   49
Leek and Bacon Penne   45
Mushroom Rissoto   51
Pasta Vongole (with cockles and
  tomato pesto sauce)   48
Pasta with Bacon, Avocado and
  Mushrooms   46
Pasta with Country Chicken Sauce   47
Pasta with Cream and variations   50
Pasta with Eggplant, Spicy Sausage
  and Peppers   44
Pasta with Pumpkin, Roasted
  Walnuts and Pesto   45
Pasta with Spinach and Feta   46
Penne with Feta, Olives, Rosemary
  and Chillies   46
Perfect Dinner Party Pasta   44
Perfect Rice   109
Pumpkin Risotto   51
Spaghetti with Artichokes, Olives,
  Tomatoes and Pesto   48
Spaghetti with Smoked Salmon and
  Green Peppercorns   48
Speedy Pasta Combinations   48

Pies, Tarts and Slices

Alsace Onion Tart   106
Anne's Spinach Tart   106
Corn, Pepper and Chilli Bake   106
Harvest Chicken Pot Pie   84
Open Filo Spinach and Feta Pie   107
Potato, Feta and Olive Slice   108
Smoked Fish and Kumara Pie   70
Tuscan Cheese Bake   106
Zucchini and Cheese Tart with
  Poppyseed Pastry   106

Prepare Ahead

Anne's Spinach Tart   106
Avial (Mixed Vegetable Curry)   110
Braised Oxtails with Red Chilli
  Beans   100
Creamy Chicken and Bean Daube   83
Duck and Mushroom Fettuccine   44
Felafels with Yoghurt Sauce   104
Gurnard with Indian Spices   54
Harvest Chicken Pot Pie   84
Mexican Fish Parcels   69
Microwave Vegetarian Moussaka   111
Oriental Fish Parcels   70
Potato Feta and Olive Slice   108
Semolina Tortini   104
Smoked Fish and Kumara Pie   70
Spicy Chicken Couscous with Roasted
  Peppers and fresh Green Beans   84
Spicy Mexican Chickpeas   110
Steak Mushroom and Kidney
  Pudding   101
Tuscan Cheese Bake   106
Vegetarian Couscous   105

Salads

Asparagus Salad with Cashews,
  Bacon and Oranges   38
Avocado, Bacon and Banana Salad   35
Brie, Bacon and Avocado Salad   37
Caesar Salad   34
Fresh Banana Salad   113
Greek Salad   113
Marinated Mozzarella with Baby
  Tomatoes and Pickled Walnuts   38
Mixed Green Salad with Roasted
  Walnuts   38
Oriental Pork Salad   36
Pawpaw, Avocado, Pepper and
  Prawn Salad   35
Raw Energy Salad   36
Salad of Garlic Prawns, Avocado
  and Beans   40
Salad of Roasted Fresh Walnuts
  and Grilled Hipi-iti   34
Spinach and Feta Salad with Olives
  and Croutons   37
Thai Beef Salad   37
Thai Smoked Chicken Salad   34
The Art of Making a Good Salad   39
Venison Salad with Watercress
  and Wild Berry Dressing   41
Warm Chicken Liver Salad   40
Warm Chicken Salad with Chilli
  Peanut Dressing   41
Watercress and Mushroom Salad   113
Winter Salad with Bacon and
  Mushrooms   40

Seafood

Barbecue Mussels and Pipis with
  Flavoured Butter   57
Caribbean Fish Rolls   55
Chargrilled Whole Fish Wrapped in
  Leaves   72
Chilled Oysters with Shinto
  Dressing   18
Chilli Garlic Prawns   65
Chilli Smoked Mussel Rice Cakes   21
Cockles or Mussels with Pesto Cream
  Sauce   61
Cooking Whole Fish   72
Crayfish with Flavoured Butter   56
Creamy Pasta and Scallops   50
Fish Fillets with Toasted Almonds
  and Lime Juice   58

Fish Steaks with Sundried Tomatoes
    and Peppers   58
Flash-roasted Fish with Pesto   54
Flash-Roasting   60
Florentine Fish Rolls   55
French Mussel and Fennel Pan   68
Fresh Fish and Vegetable Toss   67
Garlic and Lemon Squid   20
Grilled Fish Steaks with Flavoured
    Butter   57
Grilled Fish with Thai Seasonings   73
Grilling   60
Gurnard with Indian Spices   54
Hot-Roasted Whole Fish   72
How to Select and Store Fish   61
Mango Prawns from Hell   63
Marinated Fish or Scallops   20
Mediterranean Skewered Fish and
    Vegetables   54
Mediterranean Squid   58
Mediterranean Stir-fried Squid   67
Mexican Fish Parcels   69
Mussels on Half Shell with Pesto
    Vinaigrette   19
One-Dish Fish Dinners   70
Oriental Barbecue Tuna Steaks   54
Oriental Fish Parcels   70
Paella   71
Pan-fried Fish with Avocado Sauce   62
Pan-fried Fish with Spicy Cashew
    Sauce   62
Pan-fried Salmon Steaks with a Light
    Fume and Brie Sauce   62
Pan-fried Scallops or Fish Fillets with
    Flavoured Butter   57
Pan-frying   60
Parmesan Grilled Fish   59
Pawpaw, Avocado, Pepper and Prawn
    Salad   35
Poaching   60
Salad of Garlic Prawns, Avocado and
    Beans   40
Salmon Sates with Sesame
    Mayonnaise   13
Salmon Tartare   18
Scallops Cooked in the Shell with
    Flavoured Butter   56
Smoked Fish and Kumara Pie   70
Smoked Fish Fritters   17
Smoked Salmon Frittata   16
Spaghetti with Smoked Salmon and
    Green Peppercorns   48
Spicy Squid and Asparagus Stir-fry   66
Stir-fried King Prawns and Squid   66
Tahitian Fish Sandwich with Fresh
    Banana Salsa   65
Thai Fish Curry   60
Thai Shrimp Dip   12
Tuna Sashimi   18
Veracruz Fish Bake   68
Whitebait Fritters   17
Whole Baked Fish Sandwiches   65
Whole Maumau baked in Ginger and
    Coconut   72

Soup

American Mussel and Corn
    Chowder   28
Mexican Mussel Soup   28
Miso Soup   29
Moroccan Pumpkin Soup   26
Mussel Soup   28
Smoked Ham Soup with White Beans
    and Mint   26
Spicy Sausage and Chickpea
    Minestrone   26
Stocks as a Soup Base   29
Straciatella Soup   29
Thai Mussels with Chilli and
    Coriander   27
Tom Yum Soup   29
Wild Mushroom Soup   27

Stir Fries

Cantonese Chicken and Vegetables 80
Chicken and Broccoli with Blackbean
    Sauce   79
Chicken, Baby Corn and Pepper
    Stir-fry   80
Chilli Garlic Prawns   65
China Coast Beef and Vegetables   92
Fresh Fish and Vegetable Toss   67
Ginger Pork and Broccoli   92
Kashmir Chicken Stir-fry   80
Mediterranean Stir-Fried Squid   67
Spicy Squid and Asparagus Stir-fry   66
Spicy Tofu and Vegetable Toss   110
Stir-fried King Prawns and Squid   66

Sweet Treats

Apricot Almond Fudge   124
Apricot and Nut Rocky Road
    Slice   125
Chocolate and Cherry Slice   124
Chocolate Truffles   125

Techniques

Cooking the Perfect Steak   94
Making A Fruit Salad   116
Matching the Fish with the Method   60
Stir-frying Technique for Meat
    Dishes   93
The Press Test for Doneness of
    Meat   96
To Make A Gravy   97
To prepare Fish in Parcels   70

Vegetable and Side Dishes

Chilli Sesame and Coriander
    Noodles   113
Chinese Stir-fried Greens   113
Crispy Kumara Cakes   112
Dried Mushrooms   27
Fresh Banana Salad   113
Greek Salad   113
Preparing Vegetable Crudites   12
Pureed Garlic   8
Quick Potato Gratin   112
Roasted Garlic   8
Roasted Peppers   9
Steamed Bok Choy   83
Stir-fried Vegetable Medley   113
To Blanch Spinach   83
Vegetable Crudites   12
Vegetable Platter with Green Goddess
    Dressing   108
Vegetable Purees — hint box   105
Watercress and Mushroom Salad   113

Vegetarian

Alsace Onion Tart   106
Anne's Spinach Tart   106
Avial (Mixed Vegetable Curry)   110
Cashew Nut Dipping Sauce   12
Corn, Chilli and Coriander Fritters   17
Corn, Pepper and Chilli Bake   106
Crispy Vegetable Rice Cakes   21
Dark Rich Mushroom Sauce   105
Dried Mushrooms   27
Felafels with Yoghurt Sauce   104
Filo Vegetable Samoosa Parcels   108
Flash-roasted Potatoes with Peppers
    and Onions   112
Fresh Banana Salad   113
Green Goddess Dressing   108
Herb and Feta Frittata   16
Herb Pancakes with Chilli
    Ratatouille   104
Marinated Mozzarella with Baby
    Tomatoes and Pickled Walnuts   38
Microwave Vegetarian Moussaka   111
Miso Soup   29
Mixed Green Salad with Roasted
    Walnuts   38
Moroccan Pumpkin Soup   26
Mushroom Rissoto   51
Open Filo Spinach and Feta Pie   107
Pasta with Spinach and Feta   46
Penne with Feta, Olives, Rosemary
    and Chillies   46
Potato and Pea Curry   110
Potato, Feta and Olive Slice   108
Protein Complements for
    Vegetarians   108
Provencal Bean and Eggplant
    Sauce   105
Pumpkin Risotto   51

129

Pumpkin Stuffed with Tofu and Asian
  Flavourings   109
Raw Energy Salad   36
Salad of Roasted Fresh Walnuts and
  Grilled Hipi-iti   34
Semolina Tortini   104
Spaghetti with Artichokes, Olives,
  Tomatoes and Pesto   48
Spicy Mexican Chickpeas   110
Spicy Tofu and Vegetable Toss   110
Spinach and Feta Salad with Olives
  and Croutons   37
Stir-fried Vegetable Medley   113
Sushi Rice Cakes   21
Tuscan Cheese Bake   106
Vegetable Platter with Green Goddess
  Dressing   108
Vegetable Purees — hint box   105
Vegetarian Couscous   105
Vegetarian Nutrition — hint box   108
Watercress and Mushroom Salad   113
Yoghurt Sauce   104
Zucchini and Cheese Tart with
  Poppyseed Pastry   106

Acknowledgements

Photographers

Bill Nichol
Pages 10, 14, 16, 23, 28, 37, 38, 39, 41 (bottom), 45, 47, 48, 49, 55, 59, 63, 66, 71, 77, 78, 79, 81, 83 (left side), 91, 93 (left side), 95, 97, 107, 109, 111, 114, 117 (bottom)

Becky Nunes
Pages 6, 15, 19, 24, 29, 31, 32, 35, 42, 51, 52, 69, 74, 85, 88, 99, 100, 102, 119, 121

Robin Morrison
Pages 46, 67, 68, 73, 87, 93 (right), 98

Robin Morrison for Cuisine Magazine
Pages 13, 17, 41 (top), 83 (right), 101, 117 (top), 123

Ian Batchelor for Cuisine Magazine
Pages 21, 125

Stephen Robinson for Cuisine Magazine
Pages 57, 64

Bill Double for Cuisine Magazine
Page 36

Your food looks even better when presented on a range of exciting tablewear. There's no need to use a complete dinner set. Buy unusual, individual pieces to add drama to your table. We are very grateful to a number of local specialist tableware shops for providing us with wonderful serving plates and dishes.

Citrus Wood
Page 77

Fay Chandler
Large plate, page 19
Page 24
Page 32
Page 35 (right)

Harts
Page 29
Page 35 (left)

Living and Giving
Page 14
Page 28

Morris and James
Page 40
Page 81

Milly's
Page 90

The Designstore
Page 42
Page 51
Page 52
Page 74
Page 85

The Studio of Tableware
Page 55
Page 63
Page 66
Page 79
Page 91
Page 92
Page 94
Page 117

The Store
Page 67
Page 87
Page 95

Notes

Notes